W9-AMB-580

Showing Mary

Showing Mary

HOW WOMEN CAN SHARE PRAYERS, WISDOM, AND THE BLESSINGS OF GOD

RENITA J. WEEMS

West Bloomfield, Michigan

WARNER BOOKS

An AOL Time Warner Company

Scripture references are taken from the Holy Bible: New International
Version®, copyright © 1973, 1978, 1984 by International Bible Society.

Published by Warner Books, Inc., with Walk Worthy Press, Inc., 33290 West
Fourteen Mile Road #482, West Bloomfield, MI 48322

Real Believers, Real Life, Real Answers in the Living God™

Warner Books, Inc., 1271 Avenue of the Americas, New York, NY 10020

Visit our Web site at www.twbookmark.com and www.walkworthy.net.

 An AOL Time Warner Company

Printed in the United States of America

First Printing: May 2002
10 9 8 7 6 5 4

ISBN: 0-446-53066-2
Library of Congress Control Number: 2002100987

Book design by Giorgetta Bell McRee

For Cecilia,
who many years ago
taught me how to pray out loud.

Contents

❦

Contents

The Gospel According to Luke

Chapter 1 Verses 26—56

26 In the sixth month, God sent the angel Gabriel to Nazareth, a town in Galilee,

27 to a virgin pledged to be married to a man named Joseph, a descendant of David. The virgin's name was Mary.

28 The angel went to her and said, "Greetings, you who are highly favored! The Lord is with you."

29 Mary was greatly troubled at his words and wondered what kind of greeting this might be.

30 But the angel said to her, "Do not be afraid, Mary, you have found favor with God.

31 You will be with child and give birth to a son, and you are to give him the name Jesus.

32 He will be great and will be called the Son of the Most High. The Lord God will give him the throne of his father David,

33 and he will reign over the house of Jacob forever; his kingdom will never end."

34 "How will this be," Mary asked the angel, "since I am a virgin?"

35 The angel answered, "The Holy Spirit will come upon you, and the power of the Most High will overshadow you. So the holy one to be born will be called the Son of God.

36 Even Elizabeth your relative is going to have a child in her old age, and she who was said to be barren is in her sixth month.

37 For nothing is impossible with God."

38 "I am the Lord's servant," Mary answered. "May it be to me as you have said." Then the angel left her.

39 At that time Mary got ready and hurried to a town in the hill country of Judea,

40 where she entered Zechariah's home and greeted Elizabeth.

41 When Elizabeth heard Mary's greeting, the baby leaped in her womb, and Elizabeth was filled with the Holy Spirit.

42 In a loud voice she exclaimed: "Blessed are you among women, and blessed is the child you will bear!

43 But why am I so favored, that the mother of my Lord should come to me?

44 As soon as the sound of your greeting reached my ears, the baby in my womb leaped for joy.

45 Blessed is she who has believed that what the Lord has said to her will be accomplished!"

46 And Mary said: "My soul glorifies the Lord

47 and my spirit rejoices in God my Savior,

48 for he has been mindful of the humble state of his servant. From now on all generations will call me blessed,

49 for the Mighty One has done great things for me—holy is his name.

50 His mercy extends to those who fear him, from generation to generation.

51 He has performed mighty deeds with his arm; he has scattered those who are proud in their inmost thoughts.

52 He has brought down rulers from their thrones but has lifted up the humble.

53 He has filled the hungry with good things but has sent the rich away empty.

54 He has helped his servant Israel, remembering to be merciful

55 to Abraham and his descendants forever, even
as he said to our fathers."

56 Mary stayed with Elizabeth for about three
months and then returned home.

Introduction

You are on the verge of something special. You know
it. You can feel it. Something is in the air. You are restless and don't know why. You wake up in the morning
with flutters in your stomach even though your calen-
dar doesn't indicate any special meetings scheduled for
the day. Your mind is racing from thought to thought,
and you can't figure out why. A voice in you won't be
quieted, but you can't quite make out what it's saying.
You wonder if you're forgetting something, but you forgot what. Nothing has happened or is about to happen. But it is, and you sense it. It feels as though you're
supposed to be doing something, something important, but you don't know what it is. The people and
things you usually rely upon to distract you when
you're unsettled only frustrate you right now. Today is
not the first day you've felt like this. This feeling has
been coming in waves, off and on, for some time.

You're on the verge of giving birth and don't know

it. You're pregnant. No, no, no—I don't mean you're pregnant with an actual baby (unless, of course, you *are* with child!). The birth referred to here and throughout this book is of another sort. It's the sort of birthing a woman does scores of times throughout her life without recognizing the symptoms. Her interests, her tastes, her emotions, her dreams, her image of herself grow and change throughout the phases of her life, causing enormous discomfort for her and for all those who look to her for strength and guidance. She barely notices the labor pains for what they are. This pregnancy has nothing to do with whether you're married or single, nor does it have anything to do with whether you are able or not able to bear children. Young, perimenopausal, menopausal, or postmenopausal, you are never too young or too old to give birth to yourself. New parts of yourself. New dimensions to yourself. Untapped sides of you. You are like Mary of Nazareth in the New Testament gospel stories. You are pregnant with possibility.

All the time you've been thinking it was your external circumstances that needed overhauling. A new job. A new house or apartment. A new hairstyle. A new wardrobe. A new look, period. New friends. A break from the family. A new husband. A new boyfriend. A husband or a boyfriend, period. But that's not it. Those are fine for temporary relief, but they can't quiet the deeper, interior upheaval that's going on inside you. To calm those twitters, you have to first face them and call them what they are. Spiritual gestation. Outgrowing an old self, shedding old skin, and becoming a new self. Sacred labor. Holy work. Rebirth.

I recall the first time I felt my daughter kicking and stirring inside my womb, around the second trimester of pregnancy. I was in my study at home, typing on my computer. I stopped typing in mid-sentence and lost that thought. I was both mystified and petrified, fascinated and horrified, by the sensation of a human knocking about inside me. The sensation of new life stirring in the womb is called quickening. But that morning was not the first time my daughter quickened inside me. She'd been thumping and knocking about inside me for weeks before, since conception I'm told. But I didn't know it. By the time she made her presence felt that morning, around the fifth or sixth month, she'd grown large enough inside me to become an undeniable force. It's a similar sort of feeling when you feel twinges of something yet unnamed knocking about within you, evolving and stretching into being, causing you to feel restless, your mind to race, and your spiritual appetite to change. You've been pregnant for a while. It's just taken some time for you to notice. But the signs are all there. Today there's no denying the quickening sensations. You are ready to give birth to other dimensions of you.

"What do I do?" you're asking in panic right about this moment. The first thing you do is pray as Mary of Nazareth did when she said the words, "May it be to me as you have said" (Luke 1:38). Hers was the prayer of a woman on the verge of giving birth to something sacred inside, "Lord, I want what you want for my life. Let us begin." It's that simple.

Have you ever wondered why God sent the angel Gabriel to Mary months before the baby was born to tell her that the child she was about to conceive would be the Christ child? Why didn't God just wait until after the child's birth to reveal to Mary her son's true identity? God wanted Mary to have time to prepare. The preparation she had to do was not just on behalf of the baby. Women had been giving birth to babies, and figuring out how to care for them, for hundreds of thousands of years before Mary's pregnancy. Besides, there were plenty of women on hand in Nazareth to take shifts helping young mothers care for their newborns. Hers was not a culture like ours which leaves new mothers alone for months on end. God sent Gabriel because Mary needed those months to prepare for a birth of a different sort. Parts of her self had to expire and other parts be stirred to life before she could take on the incredible task she was fated for. With the birth of Jesus her son, Mary's life would never be the same. Those flutters in her stomach all those months were flutters for herself, as much as they were in antic-

ipation for her baby. The labor pains she felt that damp
night in Bethlehem as she struggled to bear down and
push her son into the world were labor pains on behalf
of her self as much as they were for his sake. Mary had
no more control over what was happening to her than
you and I have control when we wake up one morning
unable to go on playing a role we feel we've long outgrown.

Mary is me, and Mary is you. I am Mary, and you are
Mary. Whenever you feel like you're being summoned
from some deep and holy place within to journey *to*
some deep and holy place within, know that it's God
inviting you to an altar where you might encounter
God anew and yourself anew. That's spiritual pregnancy.

"But how do I know that what I'm feeling is what
you're writing about?" you're now asking. Realize first
that everything we experience in life is designed to
make us emotionally, spiritually, and intellectually
stretch and grow. Every day we're giving birth to different parts of ourselves, or ought to be. Every crisis in
our lives is used as an invitation from God to meet
God anew, and to discover new dimensions of who we
are and what we are capable of. We are continuously
moving from one stage of pregnancy to another. Some
become difficult labors, others are less so. Sometimes
the feeling that we're on the verge of something comes
and goes—and then comes back, each time with

greater intensity until we're gripped by it and unable to ignore it. But you know it is God drawing you into a birthing season when, like Mary of Nazareth, you know you can't go back to the woman you once were, but still you can't say for sure who this new woman is you're changing and evolving into. At the same time, you can't stay where you are for much longer without risking damaging the something deep and sacred that's bubbling on the inside. Next time you feel a quickening sensation, pray with Mary, *Lord, I want what you want for me. Let's begin.* Take responsibility for your own growth. God expects you to share with God in midwifing your own wholeness. If you take responsibility for your own growth, then perhaps you will become as invested as God in preserving and nurturing your self. Giving birth to yourself begins with praying, "Lord, I want what you want for me. Let us begin." That was Mary's way of saying yes to God.

"But where do I begin?" you ask. By keeping yourself open to God. That's it. Look around. Pay attention to your life. Listen for the sounds of the season. Pay attention to the people God sends into your life during this period. New friendships. Prayer partners. Role models. Mentors. Strangers who say something you can't get out of your mind. Renewed friendships. "Even Elizabeth in her old age, who is supposed to be too old to conceive, is pregnant," the angel hinted to Mary. Nothing more was offered. Mary figured it out.

She headed for Elizabeth's home. She knew not to go straight to Joseph, who would not have believed her and who would have badgered her to make sense and get to the point. Stay away from the Josephs who demand that you have answers, make a decision, and give a name to what's going on. It takes time to give birth. Find women (and men), prayer partners, mentors, friends, who know birthing pangs when they hear them being described. Partner with people who share your passion for life and for learning new things. Find a dancing partner and compose your own praise song, or Magnificat. Make up the words. Make friends as you go. You're on the right road to Elizabeth's house when you encounter the unlikeliest of people, the unlikeliest of conversations, the unlikeliest of songs and events— or when you stumble on a book like *Showing Mary*— whose timing leaves you chuckling, praying, and saying, "This can only be God."

"Greetings, You Have Found Favor"

"Greetings, you who are highly favored! The Lord is with you" (Luke 1:28). The angel's odd greeting alarmed Mary. For one thing, his was a greeting normally reserved for girls of a more noble background than her own. Rich girls were the favored ones, not poor girls from poor, working-class towns like Nazareth. Hers was not one of the tony sections of Galilee. Nazareth was a solidly working-class, unremarkable village. It was located in lower Galilee, if that tells you anything. So unremarkable were Nazareth and its inhabitants in the eyes of others throughout Galilee that upon hearing of the prophetic gifts of one Jesus from Nazareth, Nathanael, who hailed from a flossier section of town, smugly replied, "What good can come out of Nazareth?" (John 1:46). Fortunately, Jesus would learn from his mother not to be deterred by what others thought of his hometown. Mary would live out her whole life in Nazareth and would come to discover for herself that just because your background is humble doesn't mean that your future is limited. Who would have imagined an angel from heaven appearing to a poor, unsophisticated young girl from the back roads of Nazareth with an assignment from God? Mary grew up never expecting the sort of compliment paid to her that day by the angel Gabriel; afterward, however, she knew better than to ever again question God's choice.

There's no denying that Gabriel's greeting startled Mary. But hearing herself addressed directly made Mary draw back in fear even more. *"Do not be afraid, Mary, you have found favor with God"* (Luke 1:30). Imagine an angel speaking directly to a woman! Everyone knew that angels didn't communicate directly to women. But this one did. What's more, he came with news that should more properly have been conveyed to Joseph, her husband-to-be. This caused Mary more alarm. Anything affecting a woman's reputation as a bride-to-be, or anything threatening her upcoming marriage, by custom should be directed to her father or husband-to-be. Their honor as her guardians was on the line. What's more, women were not addressed directly without the consent of their fathers, husbands, or male guardians. (A few verses earlier, an angel visited Zechariahs, not Elizabeth, with joyous news of a son being on the way.) Mary was shaken by what was happening. But, she was also intrigued.

Don't be afraid, Mary, for you have found favor with God, the angel said.

"Uh-oh. Is this good news or bad news?" It's supposed to be a compliment, but it also feels like something else you have to live up to. Divinely favored. Hmmmph. It feels like you're about to be asked to do something that's going to take a lifetime to live up to. Something else added to the long list of things you already have to do. Another impossibility put upon you. Whatever plans you had for your life have been shot to pieces. No, God. Not now. Not here. Why now?

Don't be afraid, Mary, for you have found favor with God.

At the same time, it's intriguing and flattering to think that someone sees something special in you. You're tempted to question their judgment and motive. After all, you've lived your whole life around people who expected very little from your life. And let's face it, your own dreams for yourself have been rather small and conventional as well. But now someone comes along with a different forecast of your future. Says your Gabriel, "Have you ever thought about the possibility that you're more gifted than you know? You've got more potential than you suspect? You're more blessed than you think?" For example, a teacher admires your speaking and thinking skills in class and asks whether you've given any thought to applying to law school. You're speechless. It might just be that your teacher was your Gabriel. A coworker admires your competence on a project and suggests that you apply for the job that's just been posted, which pays more and would make better use of your talents. You're floored. Could that be your Gabriel? What is your reaction supposed to be? Whatever you do, don't dismiss their remarks. Hear them out. Listen for God. Search your own soul. Maybe theirs are the voices of Gabriel sent to wake you up to your own potential.

Mary could have just said no. That's certainly what you and I would have said had an angel intercepted us with harrowing news that God had decided to interrupt our best-laid plans and set us on some ridiculous course. She could have thought, *I have better things to do with my life*. She might have said to Gabriel, "No— I can't do this. My family would never accept this; you'd better find someone else to do this." Mary could have said no, and would have been in good company if she had. Moses told God, "I'm not equipped to do the job." Isaiah confessed, "I'm not good enough." Jeremiah responded, "I'm much too young." Don't we tell teenagers to just say no? But Mary didn't refuse. For once in Scripture, someone, thankfully a woman, says it right the first time. She says instead, "Let it be." How many times have we said no, wanted to say no, came close to saying no, did say no to an invitation based solely on the fact that we didn't want to be inconvenienced, ridiculed, or burdened? Give the job to someone else. Mary had her own dreams of what her future with Joseph would be like. Bringing a baby into the marriage was not one of them. Growing up so quickly and having her life changed so radically were not how she imagined her new future. But look at what Mary would have missed had she responded negatively. Besides missing the honor of being the mother of God's son, she would have missed the chance to discover new things about herself. Every time you resist God's invitation to do something new, you miss God's opportunity for you to be renewed.

So what does it mean to be favored by God? Does it mean you're different from other women, better than other women, more blessed and chosen than other women? Absolutely not. It means that you, like Mary, have God's undivided attention. You always have had God's attention. But this time you know it in ways you've never known before. You notice now that your plans have become folded and kneaded into God's plan for you. "You have found favor with God" (Luke 1:30) means that your season has come, your season to move out and step up to your potential and purpose has arrived. Your plans for yourself have not been tossed out. The favor of God now makes them possible, doable, achievable. You are now becoming ready from within. A new self is emerging. You are outgrowing the old ways. Before all attention has been on what's taking place on the outside. Your new move. Getting that child off to college. The divorce. The wedding. The promotion. The new weight loss. The new boyfriend. Now it's time to turn your attention to what's taking place inside you. Stop. Pray. Pay attention. Listen. Don't listen with your ears, listen with your heart. What are you feeling? Admit that you're both afraid and excited. What have you been wanting to do all your life but were too afraid to try? Although things have begun to swirl around you and you feel completely out of control, you can rest assured that you're on the right track, because ultimately it will all come together to your greater good. Step in the whirlwind, my sister.

O Lord, even though I cannot see my way,
still I hear your voice calling me in the whirlwind.
Things are falling apart and coming together
at the same time.
Fear and calm overtake me.
Feelings of unworthiness and divine boldness
vacillate within.
But I hear you beckoning me, telling me to get up,
reach out, look up, step out.
I hear, and I obey.

Ready from Within

Almost all change is unwilling in the beginning, even change for the best. Mary of Nazareth found this out one otherwise ordinary day in a young girl's life. The young, energetic, starry-eyed girl with a head full of nappy curls would discover firsthand both the anguish and upheaval change brings, and the excitement and potential for growth it offers. Swathed in her daydreams that day of her pending marriage within the year to Joseph, a descendant of the house of David, Mary represents every woman who knows what it's like to wake up from a cherished dream and find that her life has been turned upside down by one turn of events. Little did Mary know that day as she walked the dusty roads of her fishing village of Nazareth that her life was about to change forever. An angel appeared out of nowhere and startled her. His good news didn't much sound like good news in the beginning. According to him, she had been chosen by God for a special mission. Through her the whole course of human history would be altered. God had chosen her to conceive and bear a son for God. The seed implanted in her womb would grow to become God's beloved son on earth, whose presence would usher in a new era of salvation for the whole universe. The young starry-eyed teenage girl from a humble Nazarene household, who never dreamed of anything more exalted for herself than drinking fresh goat's milk every day and marrying a boy with straight teeth, was shocked by and unprepared for the bittersweet good fortune that comes with being nudged awake by God.

Ask any woman whose life has ever been turned upside down, even by a positive event, and she'll describe the sensation that seizes you as the earth begins shifting beneath your feet, as though you've been lurched awake out of a deep sleep. It's difficult to focus in the beginning. The light hurts your eyes. But slowly you begin looking around, and everyone and everything around you looks different. The world hasn't changed. *You* have changed. You are awake now, and the world looks different awake. But what are you supposed to do now that you're awake? For as inept and unprepared as you feel, it seems it would have been better to remain unconscious, or so you tell yourself. As much as you yearn to go back to sleep, once you're awakened you can never sleep soundly again.

Of all the women in the Bible, Mary perhaps was

most intimately acquainted with the bittersweet nature of change. Her very name, derived from the Hebrew word *mara*, means "bitter" or "bittersweet." Mara is the name Naomi chose for herself when she returned home to Bethlehem bereft of husband and sons (Ruth 1:20–21). *Do not call me Naomi [pleasant]*, Naomi hurled at those who came out to welcome her home. *Call me Mara, because the Almighty has made my life bitter*. The devotion of Ruth, her eccentric daughter-in-law, was all the older woman had to sweeten her bitter fortune. Like Naomi, Mary's life both came undone and came together with her new circumstance. Which do you do first when you wake up and come to yourself? Cry or laugh? Deny what's happened or face it headlong? Weep and pray or pray and weep?

See the world from Mary's perspective: You spend your whole life doing pretty much what's expected of you. You never allow yourself to dream too big for fear of being disappointed. You just do what you are told and keep your expectations to a minimum. One day something happens and your life is sent tumbling out of control, shattering at your feet and crumbling into a million little pieces. Your first impulse is to stoop down and scoop up as many pieces as you can and put your life back together. Quickly now before others see you falling apart and you appear unable to cope. Hurry before you forget which piece goes where.

How would you feel if this happened to you?:

You've outgrown the job you have. Your new job requires a move to a new city. Your last child moves out of your house and into his own apartment, and your cat has to be put to sleep. The guy you've been dating finally asks you to marry him. Your mother dies suddenly. You're pregnant at forty-something. The opportunity comes along to start your own business. Life doesn't look the same anymore. The world doesn't feel the same anymore, does it? Your world feels flung to the winds. It's as though everything you've pieced together in life has come undone and has been left strewn on the floor. Your first impulse? *Pick up as many of the scattered pieces as you can, rethread the necklace, and put it back around your neck*, you tell yourself. Look normal. Don't let it seem as though you don't know what you're doing. Look prepared and in control. You try, but there are so many scattered, shattered pieces. Never in your wildest dreams did you imagine yourself faced with so much upheaval. But now that it's happening, you catch yourself wondering. *What if . . . ?* Despite the overwhelming grief you feel at watching your world turn upside down with this new turn of events, you can't deny that you're curious. There were parts of your old life you never liked much anyway. Not really. Truthfully, you don't want your old life back. You feel tugged to begin a new chapter, a new life. You're petrified, but you're also excited. A side of you is scared. But another side of you has always been waiting for this moment, ready for change, open to something new. Something within is ready.

If you sense the ground shifting underneath your feet and change taking place in your life, then you are Mary of Nazareth. You know what it feels like to find yourself caught between wonder and worry, awe and anguish over all the change taking place in your life. On the one hand, you're ready and have been hoping for something as dramatic as all that's going on to help get you started on your new path. On the other hand, however, no matter how much you try to convince yourself, you're not as ready as you'd thought. As good as it is, it also hurts.

Are you ready from within for the bittersweet changes that follow when God starts moving in your life? Before Mary could handle all the changes that were about to take place in her outer world—her relationship to Joseph, an unplanned pregnancy, the scandal her pregnancy would bring upon her family, the task of raising God's son—she needed to attend to some changes already taking place on the inside. Before God permits any change to take place in our outer world, whether positive or negative, God always sends gentle nudges ahead of time to ready us from within. Pay attention! Get ready! Listen to the woman within who has been secretly waiting for Gabriel. She too loves Joseph. But she doesn't want a conventional marriage. She too is looking forward to having babies.

But she doesn't want to have to lose vital parts of herself for the sake of motherhood. In order to combat all the old stereotypes about what it means to be a woman, and in order to be the woman God is calling her to be, she needs inner confidence. She needs an encounter with the Holy. She needs an angel to come and rouse her from her sleep.

O Lord, I have been asleep for so long, but within me is a place of readiness.
I am ready to wake up. I am ready to open my eyes.
I am ready to see.
I am ready to get ready.
Even though it's difficult to focus, and the temptation is to go back to sleep . . .
I hear the alarm. I sense the new day.
I feel me coming alive in you. I feel you coming alive in me.
Let us begin, O Lord.

God Is with You

Two promises accompany the blessing of God's favor. First the angel assures Mary, "The Lord is with you." No elaboration given. No details offered. Nothing more said. "The Lord is with you." Like a mother who stands waist deep in the water with arms stretched to a toddler tottering on a pool's edge, *I will catch you*, her arms communicate. Like an adult child standing at the hospital bedside of a parent recently out of surgery but still too drugged to be roused, wiping her mother's brow, slipping socks on her feet, braiding her hair, singing her mother's favorite hymns throughout the morning, her presence is meant to communicate to her mother's spirit, *I am here for as long as it takes for you to find your way back to us*. We have God's assurance that no matter how irrational the season turns out to be, no matter how long it takes or how painful it is for us to fully come to consciousness, God is with us (or in Hebrew, *Emmanuel*).

Look back over your life at the "Emmanuel" moments you've already experienced. The car crash that could have permanently maimed you: *Emmanuel*. The marriage crisis that almost sent you over the edge (and did, but you came back): *Emmanuel*. The fire that could have destroyed everything and everyone you love: *Emmanuel*. God's assurance is that with God's favor comes God's abiding presence. This explains why the angel said, *Don't be afraid*. Startled as you may be at this turn of events, rest assured that you have nothing to fear. God is in control. You are in God's hands. A future awaits you.

The second promise of God's favor comes in the form of the gift of a friendship. God's favor always results in the gift of companionship along the journey, new friendships, sustenance in the form of co-journeyors, partners, and mentors. Have you ever noticed how much of popular spirituality emphasizes the lonely, nonrelational nature of the spiritual journey? The image conjured up in many books about the spiritual journey is that of the lone pilgrim, the cloistered, solitary novitiate, the lonely recluse, the individual believer who must go it alone on the path to wholeness. Of course, there's a fair amount of biblical support for this image. Prophet upon prophet encountered God alone on mountaintops, with nothing more than sheep as their witnesses, or stood alone in the temple, with nothing more than cherubim flying about to bear testimony to it all. Similarly, fishermen struck out on their own and left homes and families to follow a certain Galilean prophet named Jesus. It is up to women, however, to bring balance to the conversation by pointing out the more relational aspects of the spiritual journey. In Scripture, every person God singled out for service may have started out alone, but they did not end up alone. All found themselves eventually paired up with people—friends, mentors, spiritual partners—who helped nurture them along their journey. Abraham brought his nephew Lot along with him. Joseph wept at the chance to reunite with his scoundrel brothers. Samuel followed Eli around like a puppy. David counted on Jonathan. Elishah mimicked Elijah. Ruth clung to Naomi. Timothy blossomed under Paul's tutelage. Jesus enjoyed the camaraderie of his disciples. Why should it be seen as a weakness on Mary's part that she seek out the company of her friend and cousin Elizabeth when her blessing felt too much for her to bear? Why should solitude be the only path to spiritual growth? It isn't. Often just to keep the initial awakening alive, you need the support of others to help you hear your voice. Even the woman who has given herself over to a life of aloneness as part of her religious duty—the cloistered nun whose life conforms to the rhythms of the convent and the music of silence—discover hers is a life that seeks to find a balance between the solitude of prayer and devotion to

God and communion and communication with her fellow sisters in her order.

Mary had Elizabeth. Deeply tied up with Mary's call to spiritual growth and maturity was her visit to the hill country to spend some time co-journeying with her elder cousin Elizabeth. The journey from a false or old self to a new, authentic self may start off with an extraordinary event, a conversation with the supernatural. But to stay nourished and encouraged along the long, winding road, you'll find that you need real, flesh-and-blood friends, mentors, confidantes, partners to accompany you. At some point you have to open up and let someone into your dreams and visions. You have to speak them out loud to someone. Find someone who will be happy for you, someone with dreams of her own, someone who knows something of what it means to be blessed and gifted for special work. Stay away from those who resent your dreams. You need to surround yourself with Elizabeths who will hold you accountable to your dreams: "I thought you said you weren't going to keep spending, that you wanted to pay off your bills so you could return to school." "I thought you said you would never again get involved with a married man." "I distinctly recall your enthusiasm last year about this new move. What happened?"

While Mary had ultimately to grow out of girlhood and into womanhood to do what God was calling her to do, she was not alone along the journey. God sent her Elizabeth over in the next town to help her in the early critical stages of the long journey ahead. Her older cousin was already six months pregnant by the time Mary found out from Gabriel that she too was pregnant. But theirs was not a one-sided spiritual partnering. Elizabeth needed the energy and enthusiasm of her young cousin as much as the younger woman needed the wisdom and steadying strength of the older woman. Mary stayed with her cousin for three months, just enough time to see Elizabeth through her own pregnancy and the birth of her son, John the Baptist. Enough time for the older woman to allay Mary's fears that she wouldn't be able to carry through on what God was calling her to do. Enough time for Elizabeth to point out to Mary all the ways in which Mary's whole life, all her previous aches, had been preparing her for this special mission.

Mary probably returned to Elizabeth many times over her years as a young mother, though there is no mention of these visits in the gospel stories. And it's likely that she partnered with many other women along the way as she experienced transformation after transformation in her journey as a mother. Every Mary needs an Elizabeth (two, three, four Elizabeths!) who acts as a confidante, a friend, a partner, a mentor to help walk with her, especially along the bumpy parts of the journey, and if not all the way, for at least part of her journey. She is always looking for role models who might show her how to strike a balance among her many selves: the sacrificing mother, the faithful wife, the loyal friend, the devoted daughter, the quiet thinker, the eternal dreamer, the mystic believer, the wise crone, the teenage girl who never had a chance to fully be a teenager.

Look around at the women in your life. Who are the women God has placed into your life to be potential role models, confidantes, prayer partners, accountability partners? So, you live out of town, and away from all the older women you remember from your childhood. Surely there must be older women where you live. What older women, wise, praying women, godly women, do you see every Sunday in church, there on your job, next door in your community, whose womanly wisdom stirs you to good works? Perhaps the problem is that your friendships are too narrow. Make friends with women from a wide range of backgrounds. Senior citizens. Boomers. Generation Xers. Educated. Streetwise. Married. Divorced. Single. Richer. Poorer. Don't just choose your friends by those who will encourage you and tell you what you want to hear. Find a friend who will love you enough to tell you the truth as she sees it. She may not always be right, and you may not agree with everything she says. But you respect the fact that she has your best interests at heart, and that she's a praying woman.

Above all, Elizabeth is a friend, a prayer partner, a

soul mate, far enough along in her own journey that she knows about changing, transforming, growing, maturing, and shedding old layers of the self. If she doesn't have any experience with being pregnant, spiritually pregnant, pregnant with new parts of herself, then think again about pouring your heart out to her. You need a co-journeyor, not a spectator. And when you find Elizabeth, bring something to the relationship other than just your need for what she has to offer you. Befriend Elizabeth woman to woman. That is, have something to offer. Complement her wisdom with your enthusiasm. Balance her willingness to share advice with your willingness to teach her new skills. Mary came as much to support Elizabeth in her own pregnancy as to pull wisdom from her. Go find Elizabeth.

*Wherever Elizabeth is, she is not far from where
I am right this moment.
Show her to me. Show me to her. Show us
to each other.
I thank you for the loyalty and the love of the
Elizabeths I already have in my life.
Deepen those bonds so we might continue
to grow together.*

But for the secret parts of me that are on the verge
of being born,
send new Elizabeths to help midwife them and
show me how to do the same for them.
God, I am ready.

"To a Girl Named Mary"

❧

Don't let all the religious symbolism surrounding her—*Blessed Virgin, Our Lady, Mother Mary, Queen of Heaven*—confuse you. At fourteen, Mary was still only a girl. She began her journey as a frightened, young, naive girl thrust into a role she evolved into before her own eyes, just like you and me. And if you're thinking that fourteen years old is much too soon to be making decisions that will affect the rest of one's life, you're correct by the standards of our day. A fourteen-year-old girl is too young to be gripped with life-and-death questions. But fourteen is just about the age Mary was when the angel Gabriel visited her with news that she was pregnant. At fourteen years old, sixteen tops, Mary was already a bride and a soon-to-be mother. Girls in ancient cultures were usually married off to boys or men in their villages as soon as they reached adolescence, that is, as early as twelve years old, but more often around fourteen. (Twelve-, thirteen-, fourteen-, and fifteen-year-old brides are not uncommon in many parts of the world today.) In our modern Western culture, fourteen years old is much too early to be saddled with adult responsibilities, which is why it shocks and grieves us when we see teenage girls pregnant and already mothers of one, two, or more children. Their lives are just getting started. They're just children themselves. But seen through the eyes of Mary's culture, a fourteen-year-old girl is ripe for new beginnings, especially spiritual beginnings.

Girls started families so young during Mary's time because in those days the average life span for a woman was about forty years. A woman's life expectancy depended upon the number of children she bore and whether her husband had the means to allow her the best midwife care possible. Women who had lots of children, one rapidly after another, with little rest between and poor midwife care to call upon, tended to have a higher mortality rate than women who had fewer children and better midwife care. If the average life span for poor women was less than forty years, then it stands to reason that fourteen years old was half a lifetime for many females. Unbelievable as it sounds, the emotional and spiritual shock Mary experienced at fourteen can be equated with what a woman living today experiences during what's known as our midlife transitional period—say, between the age of thirty-five and fifty-five. When she asked, "How can this be?" Mary was in her own way asking, "How am I supposed to respond to this news?" She was not questioning the wisdom of her age. Instead she was questioning the inconvenience of it all. After all, she was only a teenager, no doubt feeling ill prepared for what was being asked of her. How would she explain this to Joseph? Even in ancient times, fourteen-year-olds did not relish standing out from their peers. Mary never dreamed of being so different as to challenge the social order regulating a girl's life. She knew enough to realize that being betrothed and pregnant by anyone other than the man she was to marry was dangerous in her society. "Of all the girls in Nazareth," she probably asked herself again and again, "why me?"

In God's eyes evidently Mary was not too young to begin the pilgrimage to becoming her Self. And given the times in which we live, it is never too young nor too late for a teenage girl, a young adult woman, a midlife woman to discover who she is through the eyes of the One who created her. "Why me?" "Why now?" "How am I supposed to respond to this?" "What am I supposed to do?" are healthy questions for any of us to ask when we find ourselves nudged in unconventional directions by a force greater than ourselves. We ask the questions that spring up in our heart even though it will probably be years, decades even, before the answers find their way to us.

I couldn't have been more than fifteen years old

myself when, standing over me with a hot comb in her hand, my stepmother turned my face toward her own and said, peering into my eyes, "Neetie, God's got his hands on your life." Her words were completely unexpected, and I don't recall them having anything to do with what was going on at that particular moment in my life. I was getting ready for my very first date. Nothing could have been further from my mind at that moment than what God had in mind for me. But I knew enough to keep silent. It would be years, almost twenty to be exact, before my stepmother's words would mean anything to me. It would take that long for me to work my way out of the dungeon of self-loathing, self-doubt, and low expectations I had wandered into. It took that long before I stopped looking to romance to redeem me as a woman and human being.

I look back on those days now, and the fact that my stepmother passed along her words during the sensual ritual of a mother combing, brushing, braiding, and pressing her daughter's hair is not lost on me. In an act symbolizing love, closeness, and (inner) beauty, by straightening and adorning my hair my stepmother passed down from one generation of women to the next ancient wisdom, warnings, and dreams. My stepmother saw something I could not. I remain grateful to her for planting a little seed of identity and purpose in my fifteen-year-old consciousness, even though I didn't have the foggiest idea how to grab hold of it at the time. But when I did grow up and learn how, her prophecy was there embedded in my memory waiting for me to harvest it. Sometimes it takes the mind and body years to catch up to what the soul knows already. It helps for a girl to have elders surrounding her to help her see new possibilities. You don't throw away the old, wise souls in your midst. You may need them for their ability to see what you can't see. Every girl needs her mother, grandmothers, aunties, godmothers, church mothers, and the women and older girls in their community to help them dream positive, wholesome, sustaining woman dreams for themselves.

Unfortunately, women in ancient times did not have the lifestyle choices we enjoy. Marriage, sex, and babies were a girl's and woman's primary sources of stimulation, adventure, and inspiration in ancient times. (There was also, of course, the stimulation that came from sharing other women's company, especially when they all gathered early in the morning to draw water from the same well.) Thankfully, given the options available to girls today that were completely unheard of in ancient times, fourteen-year-old girls don't have to look to having sex and having babies in their teenage years as the sole ways to experience adventure and achieve self-esteem. School, sports, travel, reading, religious involvement, civic programs, sorority functions, and a host of other activities are (or ought to be) available in their communities to help stimulate the mind, body, and spirit of girls today. We would do well, then, to be sensitive to the social context of the women in the Bible when searching for role models to lift up to our young girls. We have to see these women's lives in their own settings, just as we hope our great-great-granddaughters will see our lives in their twentieth- and twenty-first-century contexts when they look back with a scrutinizing eye upon the choices we made. Asking, "What choices did she chose for herself, given the choices available to her?" is the way we hope our daughters and nieces will judge us.

We wish Mary had had other choices. Mary may have wished she'd had other options, but she did have emotional and spiritual choices. What her story does communicate beautifully is that while a girl's social and economic options may be few, her spiritual possibilities are never lacking. Mary became a teenage mother like so many girls of her day, but God used the occasion to speak directly to Mary. To a girl named Mary an angel came. Gabriel was sent to wake up Mary to her own possibilities. With the words *Do not be afraid . . . the Lord is with you,* the angel Gabriel assured Mary that no matter how difficult the days ahead were, God promised not to abandon her. Joseph might walk away from her, but God would remain by her side. Even the women at the well might reproach her because of the rumors surrounding her pregnancy, but God would meet her at the well. Greater things were stirring in her than those that were coming unbolted all around her. Of all the pregnant girls in Nazareth at the time, the angel Gabriel brought a special kind of news to a certain nappy hair girl in the fishing village. Other girls probably had their own encounters with angels. But what Mary heard was for her ears alone. So radically different was God's claim upon her, so uniquely tailored for her circumstance, so singly meant for her ears, that it would take years for Mary to appreciate all that had happened to her.

You wake one day to discover that prayers you never prayed have been answered. Dreams you were too embarrassed to dream for yourself are unfolding before you. A path unimaginable to you and those who thought they knew you await your consent. *Why you?* Why not you?

To tend this dream I cannot sleep.
To live out this prayer I must get up from my knees,
and listen from within.
I am Mary. I am not another woman's life nor
is her life mine.
My life is in God's hand. I am open to
God's divine imagination.

I am open to my own possibilities.
Don't wake me while I'm dreaming.
Don't confine me with your low expectations for me.
Don't torture me with your needs.
Don't blind me by reminding me where I come from.
I have communed with angels.
There's more to me than meets the eye.
My name is Mary. And I am pregnant with
unnamed possibilities.

Why Now?

$\mathcal{B}$ut *why now?* Mary asked.

God's timing may seem as though it takes place "out of the blue." But it's never out of the blue. It's time. Pure and simple. It's time. It's your time. Your whole life until now has been preparing you for this moment. Didn't you notice? Didn't you recognize the mini-awakenings that sneaked up on you all those years as the brush of angels' wings across your skin? Alarm after alarm went off in your head time after time, alarms you chose to ignore or you chose to postpone by pressing the "snooze" button. Not all alarms signal fire. Some signals were only tests. They were meant to prompt you to get ready for something positive that is about to happen to you. We underestimate sometimes the impact that even a positive change has on our lives. Relax: The spiritual disequilibrium you're now experiencing may be God's way of trying to prepare you for the shifts you need to make in your life to accommodate some of the answered prayers that are coming your way.

Why now? Why not now? In some ways, you have been rehearsing for this moment for years now. Okay, so there was no way you could have anticipated all the details that come with this crisis. Granted, you don't know exactly what you're supposed to do. But you are more prepared than even you know. You're more emotionally capable of handling this than you think. You know more than you think you know, even though it doesn't feel like it right this moment as you absorb the initial shock of the news. You're stronger than you think you are. You've got more going for you than you think. You've gone through all the tiny and large metamorphoses of the past years to get you ready for what you're now facing. Why do you think you were laid off after fifteen years on the job? Perhaps that was God's way of pushing you out of the nest and forcing you to try your wings. You've been dreaming about starting your own baking and catering business. Now is the time. Take off and fly.

Your hopes of conceiving and having babies one day have been stomped out by some recent news. First you cry. And then you wipe your eyes and ask God to show you the opportunities all around you to nurture children and pass along some of that spiritual wisdom your grandmother passed down to you. Start with your four-year-old nephew who otherwise drives you nuts when you visit his family. Perhaps the reason he runs over your feet with his trucks is because he's hungry for your attention.

Why do you think you made that wrong turn back there? It wasn't because you were lost. It was so that God could show you the house that is for sale, a house that looks like the one God has been showing you in your dreams in bits and pieces, the dream house in which you envisioned you and your kids walking around from room to room, giggling and barefoot.

Why at fifty are you tormenting yourself trying to decide whether to marry this man who has come along and proposed? You've kissed enough toads to know whether this is a toad or not. You've lived without a toad long enough to know you can live without a toad. Or you've let enough good ones go to know better than to let another good one slip through your fingers. Or you've lived long enough to know now that love's a risk. You're either a gambler or you're not. What's the use in having experience if you're not going to use it? Haven't you noticed God trying to get your attention all these months? Didn't you know that that was the reason behind the flutters in your stomach and your wondering quietly to yourself, *Is this as good as it gets?* What's the use in God sending angels if you're just going to shoo them away?

It is not too early. It is not too late.
Now is the time
For me to test out my wings,
To try out my voice,
To give birth to unborn parts of my self.
I have been waiting for this moment all my life, even
before I knew myself.
On one level I have never been here before.
On another level I have been rehearsing for this
moment all my life.
Teach me what I do not know, Lord.
I am ready
from within.
Let us begin, God.

What's So Great about Being a Virgin?

$\mathcal{M}$ ention the "Blessed Virgin" and most folks know immediately to whom you are referring. Even rabid Protestants who accuse Catholics with all their Marian dogma of Mary worship admit that Mary was uniquely blessed and chosen by God for her role in bearing God's son. If she isn't to be venerated, she's surely to be honored and respected if for no other reason than that she stands out as the only woman who has ever conceived a child without engaging in sexual relations with a man. How so? Beats me. All we're told is that the Holy Spirit, God's creative power, "overshadowed her," whatever that means, and she conceived. That's it. With that, Mary was spared, uh, well, both the ecstasy and the messiness of sexual relations. God the Creator impregnated Mary without despoiling her. That alone, the church has decreed down through the centuries, makes Mary a cut above every other woman in history who has ever had a child.

Centuries of arcane theological debate have stressed Mary's *differences* from other women. Commentators have gotten away with this because what we know about Mary is actually very little. Although the New Testament writers refer to Mary many times, their focus is clearly upon Jesus, her son. The earliest New Testament writer, Paul, shows no interest in her and simply mentions that Jesus was born of "a woman" in the fullness of time (Gal. 4:4). Mark alludes to Jesus' mother and family only in passing. The other gospel writers do more justice to Mary: Matthew and Luke cast light upon her in their retelling of the circumstances leading to Jesus' conception and birth, and John reports on her role at the wedding at Cana and beneath the cross. It would be centuries later, after the church's first-century beginnings, during the next three or four centuries when Christianity's claims about Jesus' divinity and lordship were hotly debated and had continuously to be defended as its fanatical adherents sought to establish a foothold for their faith in the empire, that Mary, or more accurately her reproductive parts, would become the topic of juicy debate.

Commentators, mystics, theologians, preachers, and ordinary readers like you and me have all weighed in on the topic. Was Jesus' mother really a virgin, or might she have been raped and left too scared to let on such a fact to her proud husband? Did she and Joseph eventually have sexual relations, or was she a lifelong virgin? Was Jesus her only child, or did her womb bear other children? Might she herself have been conceived immaculately? With each debate has come the need to lift Mary up above other women, to set her apart from you and me, to make her plight different from our own. As the mother of God, she was the mother par excellence, we are told. As mothers are giving, she gave more. As mothers worry and fuss over their offspring, she worried more. As women are expected to submit to whatever role they must to please those around them, Mary submitted the most exemplarily: "May it be done to me according to your word." Even when she acknowledges her superior gifts, she takes no credit for them. In the Magnificat, her praise song to God for choosing her, a lowly girl of Nazareth, she blushes to know that "all generations will call me blessed" (Luke 1:48). She is remembered in history as the Blessed Mother. How many women can live up to her image? Of course, thousands of women have died trying. They have died physically, emotionally, intellectually, and spiritually, trying to live up to Mary's impossible image. An image of motherhood and womanhood even Mary herself would not have recognized. *Virgin mother.*

Laying aside for the moment the virtually impossible image of Mary created by church theologians down through the centuries, from the sketchy portrait of Mary drawn from the gospels one finds hints that Mary was and is every woman. Like you and me, Mary knows what it means to plan your life one way and look up one day and find it heading in a totally different direction. She is the young teenage girl from the ghetto of Nazareth who conceives a child before marriage and becomes the unwitting subject of scandal. She is the pregnant woman who must explain to her husband the circumstances of her unplanned pregnancy. She is the wife whose husband wants a divorce. She is the young mother who with her husband must flee into exile with an infant shortly after his birth. She is an ordinary woman who experiences the call to shed the shallow, external spirituality of her youth to reveal a deeper layer of spirituality that comes from within. She is a woman struggling to understand a child who is single-minded about his or her purpose and deserts the family to pursue it. She is the family member who is made to suffer because of another member of the family's subversive activities. She is a mother standing by and witnessing her son's execution as a criminal. And beyond that, she is the woman who lives to experience the fulfillment of things spoken to her decades before and to see her suffering (and that of her son) vindicated with the coming of the Spirit.

By now, Mary's beginning to look like a real flesh-and-blood woman. But what do we do about the description of her as a virgin, a mother-to-be with no sexual experience? That doesn't sound like anyone you or I know, does it? Two thousand years later, Mary's identity remains, in fact, incomplete without the word "virgin" attached to it. She is not just Mary, but "the Virgin Mary." Referring to her as "the Virgin Mary" allowed the later church to distinguish her from the other two Marys in the gospels: Mary of Bethany, sister of Martha and Lazarus; and Mary Magdalene, one of the most prominent of the Galilean women to have followed Jesus. Even though both Matthew and Luke describe her as conceiving when betrothed to Joseph (i.e., formally vowed to him in marriage but not sharing a bed with him), it seems that Paul and the other New Testament writers felt no compulsion to play up Mary the Nazarene's status as a virgin, referring to her after Jesus' birth simply as Mary, mother of Jesus. But for later writers her virginity was not just another way to designate her, it was the essence of who she was (and is). She was the mother of sacrificial love. She sacrificed sexual relations with her husband to give birth to God's son. So invested have some been in Mary's virginity that they argue that Mary preserved her virginity even after Jesus' birth, throughout her marriage to Joseph. No comment! What's clear is that for a lot of folks, Mary's virginity is essential to who she is and her qualification to be the mother of Jesus—which explains the second favorite title used to refer to her, "the Blessed Virgin."

How are you and I supposed to identify with a

woman who is so naive, pure, chaste, unspoiled, ethereal, and immaculate that there's no chance of ever becoming anything like her, given the hopelessly messy creatures that you and I are? How do you for that matter identify with a woman who sets an impossible standard for motherhood? What does Mary have in common with *real* flesh-and-blood women who scream at their children, who do engage in sex, who enjoy sex, some of whom can recall in detail the delicious sexual encounters that led to the conception of their children, women who though celibate now look forward in the future to having (lots of) sexual relations with the opposite sex? What's so great about being a virgin if it makes you untouchable and sets you apart from other real flesh-and-blood women? The truth is that there's nothing great about being a virgin if all being a virgin means is to be untouched and untouchable. Mary wasn't chosen by God because she was naive and innocent. Nor was she chosen because she was able or willing to live without physical intimacy for the remainder of her life. It's time to rethink virginity.

In ancient times the word "virgin" had a different meaning than it does now. Although there's no reason to doubt that Mary was sexually chaste when the angel Gabriel appeared to her, the word "virgin," need not refer simply to one's sexual experience or lack of sexual experience. As writers have pointed out before, in antiquity a married woman, a mother, or any sexually experienced woman could be described as a virgin. That's because the word referred not to a physical state but to a woman's psychological attitude. A virgin was a woman who still had her own inner strength. She was a woman who remained unconquered. No man, or woman for that matter, had subdued her. Even though she might be involved in a committed relationship with a man, she remained true to herself. A virgin was a woman who was still in touch with her own inner values and acted according to what she believed was true and did not allow herself to be swayed by others' approval. You have only to recall the image of virgin soil, virgin wool, and virgin oil to get the true meaning of virgin. Untouched. Unused. Unalloyed. Untouched by human manipulation. Uncorrupted by human hand.

In Greek mythology, the virgin goddesses, Artemis, Athena, and Hestia, were those goddesses who had never been seduced, raped, or humiliated by their male counterparts. Emotional bonds did not divert them from what they considered important. The married woman who remained a virgin was a woman who knew how to love a man and remain her own woman, not allowing herself to be broken, subjugated, and twisted into something she wasn't for the sake of romance. A woman who finds herself in a relationship that requires her to lose herself in order to be loved is not in love. She is in bondage. Love spells subjugation for such a woman. Mary was raised, however, to take pride in being a virgin, as did other girls in her culture. A girl's virginity brought honor to her family. Watching one's mother and other women in the family balance virginity and love was a lesson in the ancient secrets of being a woman.

Consider what new light is cast on Mary when we are forced to reckon with the possibility that God chose Mary not simply because she was humble and sexually inexperienced. Imagine what it might mean to your life if God chose Mary because God could trust that there was a part of Mary that would always belong to God and never belong to any man. Women have twisted their personalities and deformed their bodies for centuries for love. Is it really possible that we have been doing it all wrong? For centuries to be a virtuous woman has been equated with being a submissive woman. But now consider the possibility that God doesn't ask you to go brain-dead when you fall in love. Love is supposed to heighten your strength, your creativity, your imagination, your resolve, and your dreams, not diminish them. It's supposed to awaken you to what you can do, not hem you in by telling you what you can't do. Mary the virgin looked forward to marriage to Joseph because she knew who she was. She was still very young, of course, but the seed was there. She was chosen because she had the inner strength and confidence to find her way. The world was spinning beneath her feet after Gabriel's announcement, but presumably she had the examples of other virgin women at home and in Scripture to help her get her footing back.

Recall the story of Jephthah's virgin daughter, who asked her father for permission to gather her girlfriends together for a private good-bye and mourning celebration when it became clear to her that she was fated by her father's hand to be a sacrifice to God (Judg. 11:29–40). The unnamed virgin daughter asked specifically for two months with her girlfriends away on the mountain so she and they could *lament her virginity* (Judg. 11:37). The thought of never experiencing the pleasure of lying next to a man sexually spent and transported is admittedly a sad prospect. But sadder still is the prospect of surrendering your strength and wholeness to someone you love and trust, only to be betrayed by that person. Loving a man who loves his reputation more than he does you is lamentable and warrants time away in the healing presence of sympathetic friends.

Virgins in the Bible were often the target of some men's most violent fantasies. A virgin aroused a man's masculinity. They made the best wives not only because they were sexually inexperienced and pure (meaning the men could be certain that their offspring were legitimate heirs). Virgins were prized because they were self-sufficient, strong, thinking women who were not easily conquered. Capture a virgin, so went male logic, and you've captured a spirited partner.

Imagine what it might mean if Mary the virgin girl from Nazareth captured the attention of God and was chosen to bear the Christ child because of her inner strength. God depended on her to remain emotionally, psychologically, and spiritually whole and focused through the trials and challenges that were certain to face her as the mother of God's son. If that's the case, then Mary was acting neither impulsively nor was she being a bossy mother when at a wedding in Cana just outside of Nazareth she urged her son to perform his first public miracle (John 2:1–11). Mary knew better than her son that it was time for him to get about fulfilling his mission. She had known about his divine mission longer than he had known about it.

Even her conversation with the angel Gabriel when she first discovered that she was pregnant suggests that Mary was not humble and modest to the point of being pin-brained. A bit confused by the angel's announcement, like any of us would have been, she focused on the question any virgin would have asked, "How can I have a baby when I've had no intimate contact with a man?" This is an impossibility.

The thought of immaculate conception was far-fetched even for someone brought up in a world that believed in communicating with angels. Mary was a sexually inexperienced young girl, but she was not unintelligent. She wanted to understand. She knew instinctively that such a miracle would transform her life permanently. For starters, what would it mean for her and Joseph, and how on earth would she explain this to him? Marrying a virgin, she knew, was important to a man's honor.

The angel assured Mary, "The Holy Spirit will come upon you, and the power of the Most High will overshadow you. . . . For nothing is impossible with God" (Luke 1:35–37). In others words, "Rest assured: This is the work of God in you, Mary." In short, God can use virgins. You belong to God. Trust God even when you cannot track God. Do you think Mary understood at that moment all that was taking place in her life? Do you think she comprehended fully at that moment the mission of the son she was carrying? I doubt it. Just like you and me when news comes that shakes us to the foundation, Mary was trying not to panic. She trusted God, just like you have to trust God. *With God, nothing is impossible*. There are some things you will just have to leave in God's hands. It's enough for you to stay sane, focused, and prayerful. The rest is in God's hands.

To the outside world, convincing Joseph that Mary wasn't an adulterer, comforting her family in the midst of a public scandal of having an unwed pregnant daughter, getting her through an unplanned pregnancy, and showing a girl from Nazareth how to raise a son of divine destiny, all seemed impossible. But God was up to the task. Nothing is beyond God's control. Like Mary, you can't imagine how it will work itself out. But God knows. After all, Joseph too is a part of God's plan, and so are your family, your friendships, the new thing growing within you. Rest in the fact that you are not the only one who is pregnant. Everyone close to you is pregnant too, whether they want to be or not. They too have their own amount of stretching, shedding, and growing to do. Leave it to God. Given the right time and the right environment in which to blossom, the young, inexperienced virgin girl from Nazareth would grow in wisdom and maturity enough to be able to handle the gift of God entrusted to her. Given the right time and the right environment, those around you will adjust even if right now they go stomping out of the room, slamming doors, yelling across the breakfast table. It's only labor pains. God has confidence in everything you've learned as a virgin. Concentrate on what matters most. Hold fast to what you know is right for you. Every woman who has ever succeeded in her goal of becoming a whole person, someone with purpose and direction in her life, has had to withdraw within for periods of deep concentration and meditation, and not let herself be swayed by the views, bribes, and outbursts of those around her.

Imagine a woman who has never been obsessed with
other people's opinions about her.
God, how can I have lived all these years and have
never known such freedom?
Imagine a woman who has never been
humiliated by romance.
Is such a woman alive?
Imagine a woman who is one-in-herself.
O God, is it true that it's not too late?
Is it true that I can find her again?
That she hasn't abandoned me?
She's waiting for me to come to my self?
A virgin. Me, a virgin—again? Me, intact—again?
Me, whole—again? Me, unafraid—again?
Yes, I can see it. Yes, I can feel her. Yes, I remember
her. Me, a virgin.
Me, pregnant with myself once again.
Ah yes.
Now I know what you mean . . .
The Holy Spirit would come upon me.
I found God in my Self,
and I love her.

"Pssst . . . You're Pregnant"

❧

What happens when a conventional woman married to a conventional man discovers that she is pregnant with new possibilities and it becomes evident that she is outgrowing her old way of being and doing? Brace yourself. There's bound to be a fair amount of explosion in the relationship. No one likes it when the rules change mid-game. But people are not like game rules that remain fixed and static. People change, and so do relationships. Or at least, they should.

Luke is absolutely silent about what happened when Joseph discovered that his darling, beloved fiancée was pregnant before their marriage. Matthew is equally silent except only to say that once the news broke, Joseph was a just man who resolved not to expose Mary. He set out to dissolve the betrothal quietly and be done with his relationship with Mary (Matt. 1:18–20). That would make him a proud but reasonable man in the eyes of most readers. Exactly how

Joseph found out is never stated. Did Mary break the news to him herself? Did she persuade Elizabeth to tell him instead? Perhaps Zechariah, Elizabeth's husband, agreed to have a man-to-man talk with the younger man. And once Joseph found out, what did he say? What did he do? We don't know. The reader is spared seeing a man emotionally unravel before their eyes and explode upon discovering, or suspecting, that his beloved virgin of a fiancée has betrayed him by sleeping with another man. As reasonable as Joseph comes off in the New Testament gospels, you can be sure, however, that he was a conventional Mediterranean man. In the Mediterranean world in which he lived, a man's honor meant everything to him. Indeed, maintaining one's honorable position in the eyes of the community was the driving force of every man. Deeply tied to that honor was a man's ability to maintain, protect, or avenge the sexual purity of the women in his household. A promiscuous wife, daughter, sister, niece, cousin, or fiancée brought dishonor upon a man's household. And the laws were clear on the matter. A woman discovered to have been sexually promiscuous before marriage should be stoned to death (Deut. 22:13–21). The same applied to an adulterous wife. Joseph was a just and decent enough man to spare his fiancée the threat of being put to death, but he was too conventional a man to consider the possibility of attaching himself to a woman pregnant before marriage.

It wasn't until an angel appeared to him in a dream and reassured him that Mary had not betrayed him, that the child was the result of God's intervention in Mary's life, that Joseph backed off from his plans to divorce Mary. In fact, after discovering what God was doing in his wife's life, Joseph did not touch his wife sexually until after she gave birth, says the gospel writer Matthew (1:25). Though the image we get is of Joseph as a God-fearing man who accepted God's plans for his wife, he was still a man of his times. There were moments when Joseph longed for an uncomplicated marriage, a wife he understood, a future he had some say over. Joseph wanted the woman he once knew before all this talk about angels, destiny, and being overshadowed.

But a woman wakes up one morning and discovers she's pregnant. Perhaps she is pregnant with a child. Perhaps she is pregnant with giving birth to herself. She's happy, she's terrified. She's excited, she's filled with dread. She grows larger each day, she becomes more contemplative with each new phase. This is not the way she had planned it. She's secretly excited. It couldn't have occurred at a more awkward period in her life. It was now or never. If there were only herself to consider, the decisions might be easier, the transition less stressful. But there are others to consider. Others who have grown accustomed to someone who is not pregnant. They want the old Mary back. She spoke her mind, perhaps. But she didn't have much follow-through. The Joseph isn't willing to make the shifts to accommodate the new Mary that has emerged. He sets out to put as much distance between her and him as possible.

What makes shedding the old and growing into a new self so difficult is that when you begin changing, you don't do so in isolation. You wake up, and the people you're closest to have a degree of waking up to do also. You're not the only one expecting new life. Everyone close to you is pregnant too, whether they want to be or not. Things were not turning out the way Mary had dreamed. Her life had been turned upside down by the angel Gabriel's unexpected announcement. She was pregnant, and the one-year betrothal period to Joseph was not over. How would she tell him? How would he react? Who would believe her? She was no longer simply Mary of Nazareth, betrothed to Joseph. She was Mary, mother of the son of God. She was Mary, cocreator with the Divine of new beginnings. In addition to the baby latching onto her insides, a new identity, a new self, a new woman was gestating in Mary.

It's pretty clear that Mary's not the only one who has to adjust to her new state. Everyone she's closest to has some adjusting to do as well. Everyone who loves her, needs her, relies upon her, looks up to her, or expects something from her must adjust, along with her, in what they can expect and demand from her. Ask any woman who has even changed her hairstyle without telling anyone or veered from her routine of coming straight home from work and stopped to have coffee with a friend for a few hours, about the reaction you're apt to get when you step outside the box. The ground has shifted under everyone's feet. The world is a little less safe because of your actions, or so it seems. There are always people around who are invested in the old woman, the conventional woman, the predictable woman, the virgin that's not pregnant.

In the conventional world a woman's personal spiritual journey, goals, and ambitions are encouraged only to the extent that they do not interfere with their mates, their family, and others who depend upon them. The virtuous woman (of Prov. 31) is the one who spends time overseeing, overnurturing, and overmanaging the lives of everyone but herself. Once released of feeling that she isn't a good Christian woman, Christian mother, Christian wife, Christian daughter, or Christian friend if she doesn't exhaust herself in living up to everyone else's expectations, a woman is on the path to claiming her own soul and having a life she can get excited about.

Notice that the angel brought the news that Mary was pregnant directly to Mary. He spoke directly to her ears and heart. He didn't bother telling Joseph, says the gospel writer Luke. (Matthew suggests that it wasn't that easy. Joseph needed a little cajoling from the Lord to come on board.)

I've already pointed out that in Mary's culture, women were not addressed directly by strangers of the opposite sex. That applied to male angels addressing human females too, evidently (hence Mary's reaction upon hearing the angel address her so familiarly). A few verses earlier, Elizabeth's pregnancy was announced to her husband Zechariah (Luke 1:8–21). Similarly, in Genesis, the angels brought news of Sarah's impending pregnancy not to Sarah but to Abraham as he sat outside his tents at the oaks of Mamre (Gen. 18:1–15). Any communication to a married woman was transmitted through her husband or a designated male guardian. Any communication to an unmarried girl had to be done through her father, brothers, or a designated male guardian. I hardly think that the fact that Mary's marriage to Joseph had not been consummated was the reason the angel spoke directly to her. In the eyes of her ancient Jewish culture, Mary already belonged to Joseph by the time Gabriel found her.

So why did the angel speak directly to Mary and not go through Joseph, as was the custom? We are not told. But it probably had something to do with the fact that Mary would play an important role in her son's life throughout his ministry, including his death, and even after his death. She would urge him to perform his first public miracle. She could be seen standing at the foot of the cross when he was executed. And she would be numbered in Acts 1:14 among those in the upper room devoting themselves to prayer, awaiting the dawning of the Holy Spirit. What Mary was about to cocreate with God was more than an infant, as precious a gift from God as that is. She was about to become the mother of God's divinely appointed son. Furthermore, she was giving birth to new, unused parts of herself, parts of herself she would surely need to face the uncertain future that awaited her. That didn't make other women's pregnancies any less than Mary's, or Mary's pregnancy more important to God than those of other women in Galilee. It made them different.

I envy Mary. At least she had a name for what she was going through. She was pregnant, literally and figuratively. She lived in a world that believed in visitations from angels. Our world is not so simple. What do we call those of us who feel ourselves out of sorts, restless, who are circling without landing, stumbling around without direction, weepy, agitated, half the time not certain what we're feeling, tied to a self that no longer fits, bullied by those we are in relationships with to remain the same, anxious to get started but all the while uncertain as to what we're supposed to be doing? "Pregnant" is hardly the word others would use to describe us. "Depressed," "hysterical," "looney," "emotional," and "premenstrual" or "menopausal" are the more likely terms. And that is also the way we've been taught to think about ourselves.

No one thinks that there may be parts of our selves yearning to blossom, to come alive, parts we've long suppressed, silenced, or forgotten. It would help to be able to explain what's going on inside us. It would help if we knew a name for it. Until recently, there has been none. Not really. Only in recent times have women taken up their pens and reclaimed their right to describe for themselves what's going on inside them. Spiritual awakening. Midlife crisis. Finding one's voice. Coming into one's own. Growing up. Waiting. Shedding. Transitioning. Conversion. Tapping into the goddess within. Loosening the Wild Woman. The Season of *Unknowing. Whatever.* While we're learning not to be afraid of the transformation within, it hurts nevertheless. And it hurts to see our loved ones hurting too as they long for the old woman, the old mommy, the daughters we used to be, the wife he married, the woman they hired. They hurt as they are made to sit by, watching in horror, as we thrash about trying on new ways of being and shedding the old layers of being. Pregnancy is the best metaphor to describe what we're going through. And everyone closest to us is pregnant along with us. They too will have to find their way.

And now comes the question on everyone's mind: Why do some relationships survive a woman's spiritually coming into her own, while others do not? Some Josephs do walk away, and not so quietly as the one in the Book of Matthew. Some family members never adjust. Some friends are forever resentful and bitter about your change. That is the risk. And not every woman can stand putting those around her through it. You may be the one who feels tempted to suppress what's going on inside you. You want to stifle the scream. You pretend nothing has changed. You don't know if your relationships can survive your changing. Why do some relationships survive and others do not? you ask. Some don't survive because there was never enough there in the first place, never enough "wick" in the candle (is the way one writer put it), to catch and sustain the light that's beginning to take hold.

For a conventional man, a conventional marriage, a conventional family, a conventional relationship to see a woman through spiritual growth and change, there must be an openness to grow with her, to adapt, to meet God anew for oneself. The problem with conventional marriages, conventional parenting, or conventional family dynamics is that there are usually fixed expectations and rigid roles assigned, especially to women. Whether spoken or assumed, certain obligations fall to the woman *because* she is a woman, and those obligations require her to be constantly available to meet everyone else's needs. For her to spend a day in solitude, mulling over nothing in particular but the sound of her thoughts, is a crime against her family. For her to suggest that God may be the cause of her feeling the need for time alone, the need to go back to school, the need to have friends of her own, the need to stay put for the next two hours, finishing up a good book and not answering the phone or fixing dinner for others, is blasphemous. Some of us, however, wake up one day and realize we can't continue lying down and waking up and spending our lives rearranging the furniture in suffocating rooms anymore.

The woman who opts to stifle what's going on inside her, who prefers to go back to sleep rather than to awaken to her potential, is the woman who fears there isn't enough of anything solid, grounded, *sacred* in the relationship to survive the ground shifting that takes place when God speaks.

But now the tiny key: If you can't go back to being the old woman you were once, yet you can't quite say at this point what the future holds for you, then you know you're on the verge of giving birth to something new within you. You've outgrown your old self. And a new self is whispering to you from the shorelines of your soul. The writer Anne Morrow Lindbergh poignantly captured this moment in a woman's life in her book *Gift of the Sea* when she wrote, "I must find a balance somewhere, or an alternating rhythm between these two extremes; a swinging of the pendulum between solitude and communion, between retreat and return."

There is no rushing what's going on inside. You can only wait. See it to term. Part of what it means to be pregnant is arriving at a point in your life when you crave balance. Time with self and time with others. Time with angels and time with people who nourish you, like Elizabeth. Time in communing with God and time communing with others. Time alone with one's own thoughts, and time bumping around with others dashing here and there. The biggest challenge is learning how to spend time with God so that you can spend time with others, and not allowing yourself to be gobbled up by others' expectations. It seems to take decades for a woman to learn that being comfortably alone with one's self flows from satisfying experiences of being with others, and conversely being with others is precisely what fuels a continuing longing to be alone without feeling unglued. Often it is only when a woman reaches midlife, when her childbearing days are all but over, that she learns what pregnancy is really all about.

It took me a while, but now I know.
I recognize the signs.
The agonizing restlessness, the yearning for Aloneness
without wanting to be alone.

I'm on the verge of new chapters in my life.
I can't go back. I already know what's back there.
I am not that woman anymore.
I am reeling from holding in the new woman.
We'll all have to make the adjustments.
No more shutting myself up.
No more letting others shut me up.
It's time to get into position.
And we'll need all my strength to see this birth through.

I Have Been
Here Before

❧

It's already been pointed out: God's timing is never convenient. It's either too soon or it's too late, according to human calculation. You wake up one day seeing your life in a totally different light. And you wonder how long it has been this way. Why haven't you noticed before? You find yourself looking around at the choices you've made, the relationships you're in, the things you've accumulated in your comings and goings, and you wonder if this is pretty much all there is to look forward to in life. And if it isn't, why hasn't this bothered you before? Or, if this is as good as it gets, why can't you leave well enough alone? *What's prompting me to think about this?* you ask yourself. This is no time for melodrama. This will just have to wait until a more convenient time. The phone is ringing. Grades are due. Your wedding anniversary is around the corner. Your Pap smear came back abnormal. Your son's championship hockey game is this afternoon. Your best friend just miscarried. This can wait. Whatever it is.

You may suppress the questions today, but they will return with a stronger punch later. They start off as a nudge, but left unattended they sneak back up on you and cuff you. You don't have to come up with all the answers, but they do insist that you stop what you're doing and take them seriously. Don't be taken by surprise by how insistent certain questions that spring up from your soul can be. We've spent much of our lives believing that we are human beings who happen to have a spiritual side, when the truth is that we are spiritual beings who happen to be cloaked in human form. Glimmers of our spiritual essence spring up between the cracks in our humanity and take us unaware. And we are surprised by their force.

You will experience many such moments of spiritual awakening during your lifetime. Whenever you begin asking questions, trying to figure out your place in the universe—*Who am I? Why am I here? What am I supposed to be doing? Is this all there is to life? Why do I feel so restless? How do I want to live out the second half of my life? Where do I go from here?*—you are inching your way toward prayer, the lifeline to the spiritual life. "Deep calls to deep" as Psalm 42 puts it. The holy beyond you is reaching out to the holy within you, which is opening up to experience the Divine. A patch of carpet is being laid for the entrance of mystery.

Whether you believe in prayer or not, whether you pray regularly or not, anytime you ask, *What more am I supposed to be doing with my life?* you lift your eyes to heights beyond yourself to envision a possible new and different Self. We do not so much step out of the world when we pray, rather we see the world differently. Prayer takes the mind out of the narrowness of self-interest, and you begin to see the world in the mirror of the divine.

Mary's response to the angel's announcement, "How can this be?" was an invitation for God to linger with her a little longer. Her question was her prayer. She was perplexed. She was curious. She was mystified. She was horrified. But above all she was afraid. Getting pregnant now was no small matter. This was a life-or-death matter.

"Of all times, why now?" is a prayer we're all familiar with. It's the universal spiritual prayer, in fact. "Couldn't you have found a better time than now? Why did you wait until now? God, how could you do this to me at this point in my life?" On the surface of it, God's timing is never right. It's always an impossible time, given the situation you find yourself in. Too young. Too old. Too overburdened already. Too unprepared. Too far along. Too much, too soon. Too little, too late. You wonder whether you have what it takes to face what's ahead. Your protests, your inquiries, your amazement, your shock, your fears, your expressions of wonder—all are being woven together into a garland of prayer. In fact, prayer is like a woman who walks through a garden collecting lilies, roses, and rare flowers, plucking them one by one, and weaving them into a garland of prayer she presents to her Creator. The farther along she walks in the garden, the more flowers she gathers, and the more she has to stop and unweave the garland and reweave it, each time incorporating new strands, new flower combinations. All her prayers are wrapped in the garland, but the answer to her prayers can only be gotten as she continues her pilgrimage through the garden.

Prayers are answered as you continue along the pilgrimage. You step out. You follow the questions to where they lead you. Take a hard look at where you're headed. Now take a look at where your heart wishes to go. Don't be afraid. The Gardener is with you. The Gardener knows where all the flowers are planted and which ones are supposed to lead you to which new bed of flowers.

It just has to be God who stirs us so and urges us along even when we're feeling terribly lost, inadequate, and disoriented. Losing one's direction, experiencing panic, losing one's sense of purpose, being confused, unable to explain to those closest to you what's going on, searching for which way to go, looking for markers to help you decode the path, reaching out for companionship along the journey—all of this is just how Mary felt. A sense of dread and fear about the "unnamed" crept into her bones as she felt challenged to stretch and grow, to upset her betrothal contract with Joseph's family, to risk bringing shame upon her unsuspecting husband, and to wrap her mind around something that felt alien to her way of seeing the world and herself in it. You know Mary's predicament. You sit down to calculate the losses and gains already, only to discover that to take the next step in your journey you may have to risk shedding something even more dear and precious to you. But you also stand to gain lost parts of yourself, unused parts of you, undiscovered gifts you have, things your heart warns you that you'll sorely be in need of along the road.

It just has to be you, God. Too much doesn't make sense.
And yet everything makes sense.
Everything feels out of kilter. And yet everything is in Divine Order.
It just has to be you, God.
The only way to know for sure is to keep putting one foot in front of the other.
I won't know standing in the same place.
Hmmmm . . . I wonder what's on this path. I believe I'll follow it and see where it leads me.

"Let It Be Done According to Your Word"

$\mathcal{M}$ary is every woman who has ever awakened and not been able to go back to sleep. Your life is in upheaval. Even though you can't bring yourself to ask outright, you already know the answer to the question "Will my life ever be the same again?" Even though the opportunity to grow and to improve one's life is there, there's no denying that feeling bewildered and frightened could last for a long period. The best thing you can do is to learn to accept the change you can't do anything about. Accepting change, however, doesn't mean simply lying down, doing nothing, and letting the tides of what's happening wash over you. It means accepting the fact that some decisions are out of your control. The decisions others make may impact your life, sometimes even in negative, heartbreaking ways. But their decisions don't have the power to alter the essence of who you are. For example, downsizing at your company may leave you temporarily jobless and financially strapped. But being jobless doesn't change the fact that you're gifted and that God has a purpose for your life. Nothing jolts you awake like some sort of change taking place in your life. As for the change you do have some control over, seize every chance that comes along to change your life for the better. You're the only one who can change you. Don't abdicate your power. Don't pull the covers over your head and try to go back to sleep. Follow Mary's example. Listen and learn to see yourself the way God sees you. Mary's response was, *May it be done to me as you have said.* The more popular way of translating her reply is "Let it be," which was not just another way of saying "Whatever" in that cynically resigned way teenagers of today use the expression to silence and dismiss the voice of authority. Mary only acquiesced after she felt assured that she would not have to face the uncertainty of the future alone. God was with her.

Gabriel assured Mary as best he could. "This is the work of God in you, Mary. . . . The Holy Spirit will overshadow you. . . . Nothing is impossible with God." There was no reasoning with angels, Mary probably thought to herself. It was a preposterous announcement, too preposterous to understand. But something told her to hear the angel out. She did not understand fully, but she had heard about the Holy One of Israel from her mother and the other women of her family, and all the wondrous deeds the Holy One had done on

behalf of Israel in the past. This god was not to be un-
derestimated. The whole universe was filled with
God's wonder. Besides, it was the "Nothing is impossible with God" that got to her. She knew that was true.
Mary was young, frightened, and perhaps a bit horrified that she'd been chosen to carry such an important
seed. But she'd heard her mother and other women
sing songs and tell stories about the sacred past enough
to know something about the ways of Israel's God.
There was the story of the miraculous parting of the
sea, which women throughout the land continued to
celebrate in song, dance, and with tambourine in
memory of Miriam and the other women with her
(Exod. 15:20). Then there were the stories of how in
times past the God of Israel had opened the wombs of
barren women such as Sarah, Rachel, and Hannah.
These sacred stories were passed down from one generation to the next by women in the community.

Mary knew instinctively how to acquiesce to the
Creator of the universe. "Let it be . . ." she whispered.
In other words, *Your will is my will. I want what God
wants for me. Let us begin.* What else could she say?
How do you refuse God and expect to return to your
life as though nothing out of the ordinary has taken
place? How do you refuse God and live with yourself?
When the angel departed, Mary knew that what was
happening to her was part of something larger than
herself. "The Holy Spirit will overshadow you," the

angel said. At the moment she allowed herself to listen, really listen, to the angel's voice, Mary began conceiving. The angel was gone, but the hair on her neck tingled from the strange feeling coursing through her body as she replayed the encounter in her mind. She now knew beyond a shadow of a doubt that the God of her mothers was now her God too.

You have two choices when you're confronted with some sort of change in your life. The first response is to decide to stand steadfast in your slippers and refuse to give in to the forces tugging at you. Of course, you do so at your own peril. Because one thing is for certain: If you don't respond to the first gentle nudge or sign that something needs confronting, or that things are changing, the next set of alarms will increase in intensity and disruption. In fact, some women spend their whole lives trying to avoid change. They deny the changes taking place all around them. They pretend not to see the changes taking place in themselves, in their marriages, in their children, in their parents, in the world around them. They are invested in the world as they remember it or as they created it for themselves. Change is an intruder upon their most cherished delusions. Their world has to crumble and come crashing down around their golden slippers for them to stir awake.

Others don't deny change as much as they try to protect themselves against change. They succumb to the unwritten rule for whenever change is on the horizon: Fix it, take care of it immediately, do what you can to protect yourself against its disruptions, and get your life back to normal. Unlike the other group that pretends they don't hear the alarm, this group manages to rouse themselves to respond. But it's usually a quick flick of the wrist to turn off the alarm so they can go back to sleep. Do whatever needs to be done, just so we can get back to normalcy. Sometimes that may be possible, but often it's not. One of the things about change is, it comes along and completely redefines what normal is. The possibility that after things fall apart and life comes back together again, something new, better, spectacular, fulfilling, more satisfying, and more holy can be put in place is difficult for either kind of woman to imagine.

The second response to the changes in your life, the response Mary of Nazareth chose, is to act on the invitation to grow and to accept the opportunity to discover gifts, talents, and strengths hidden within you. Mary's response, "May it be done to me according to your word," was not the response of some helpless, dutiful, mindless, submissive woman, as some would have it be. The words "Let it be" have been held up for centuries as the ideal reply of the virtuous woman to circumstances in her life. But Mary was not as helpless and as inexperienced as she's been made out to be. Nor was she quite as passive as others have made her out to be. Mary knew a preposterous promise when she heard one. News that she was pregnant without any sexual contact with a man was as preposterous as it gets. The angel had some explaining to do. "How can this be?" she asked before she ever uttered the words "Let it be." Mary asked the question, but little did she know that the answer would be as nonsensical as everything else around her.

The important thing to keep in mind is that with change comes the invitation to embark upon a journey, a pilgrimage, start a new chapter, confront some issues you need to address. Everything feels out of sorts in the beginning. And it is. But there's something there for you if you don't panic. Learning to ride out feeling bewildered and frightened and tapping into this opportunity to grow is vital to the health and wholeness of every woman, because no matter who you are, there is no escaping change.

You've spent your whole life trying to keep things together, pretending not to see what you saw, making excuses for the way things were, trying to avoid the inevitable. One day you woke up exhausted and spent, unable to keep up the pretenses any longer. Your decision to wake up made you a traitor in the eyes of those around you. But for the first time in years, you feel lighter and charmed by the possibility of a new way of living awaiting you. You feel relief, despite the fact that you don't have a clue what to expect next. *Relax and let go*, you tell yourself. Is this you?

Or maybe you're the woman who is in the throes of taking on a role she's rehearsed for all her life. The time comes to assume your new life and something happens—it's not what you thought. You're as ready as you'd hoped, but something is missing. You need someone to talk to. You're not sure where to turn. But you know you have to start somewhere. *Relax and see where God directs you*. . . .

When after years of living your life one way, you wake up one day, like Mary, and start defining yourself, questioning authority, and taking measures to redirect your life, just know that you are at risk of being accused of disrupting the divine order. Some women can't stand being ridiculed by others. They want to please. They can't take being isolated, however temporarily, from those they love. Setting their own course for their lives, especially with little direction as to how it's done, is too much to contemplate. But other women, like Mary, get up and strike out for help and advice. Despite waves of fear and dread that characteristically come crashing down upon them as they find themselves groping about for a steady grip, they muster the energy to set about finding support, role models, partners, resources to help them steady themselves for the journey ahead. They feel pressured to get up. Go. Where? Wherever one finds other women pregnant with possibility and showing.

"May it be done according to your word" does not mean that you sit passively waiting for something to happen for you. You acquiesce and agree to begin working with God in changing your life. You start paying attention. You begin seeking out relationships that will help you start awake. You are saying to God, "This may hurt for a while, but I want what you want. Let us begin."

Teach me, O God, how not to apologize for what's taking place within me.
Teach me how not to rush to protect others from the work they too must do.
It hurts. But I will survive the hurt. We all will survive the hurt.
These are only labor pains.
They are not forever.
I can't wait to be born.

Even Elizabeth

But how can I be sure that this is God? Mary never quite got the question out of her mouth, but the angel could probably tell from the expression on her face what she was thinking. The pregnant virgin needed confirmation that it was possible. She wanted to be sure that it was worth it. She wanted to know that God was indeed with her.

But how can I be sure that this is God? This one has to be the most asked question in a woman's spiritual awakening. *I don't want to make a fool of myself. I don't want to be wrong. I don't want to upset everyone with the changes I'm about to make in my life if this isn't really you, God.* It's called fleecing God. Gideon the prophet demanded proof before he set out any further in his campaign against the Midianites. To make certain that he was hearing God right, he asked God to send him a sign. He laid out a fleece of wool on a threshing floor. If there was dew on it the next morning, while the ground around it was dry, he would take that as a sign that he'd heard God right (Judg. 6:36–40). Fleecing God—we all do it. "God, if this is really you, then you go ahead of me and smooth things out with Mom before I get there." "I tell you what I want you to do, God: I'll blindly open my Bible, and if it opens to verses having anything to do with what you've asked me, I'll know this is what I'm supposed to do." We want certainty. We want proof. We want confirmation. And God wants faithfulness. But God knows that although we're spiritual beings in human clothing, our mortality sometimes gets in the way of our surrendering completely to God. The fact that we're simultaneously intrigued and repelled, confounded and curious, frightened and excited by the unknown proves that our reactions to God's tug are not simplistic.

But God knows that we sometimes need more to go on to begin the scary task of peeling back our false selves. And God has a knack for sending the right people at the right time to help embolden us and encourage us along the way. People come in and out of our lives all the time, for sure. But there's something about having the right person step into your path at the right time, bringing with them the exact prayer, insight, wisdom, and words of encouragement you needed, just when you were about to throw up your hands and demand that God give you your old unhappy life back. It's all in the timing.

"Even Elizabeth."

That Elizabeth was pregnant at all was pretty remarkable all by itself. Mary's cousin was old by ancient standards, too old to bear children, which would make her anywhere past her late thirties. After more than twenty years together, both Elizabeth and her husband, Zechariah, had long given up their hopes of having a child of their own. *"Even Elizabeth . . ."* the angel said.

Elizabeth's pregnancy shows that no matter how unbelievable your situation seems, no matter how unfathomable it all sounds, another woman somewhere is experiencing her own share of holy chaos as she stands by, just like you are, watching her life come undone. Talk to other women and see. You'll discover that you are not alone. You are not the only woman who hears God's voice in the ocean waves. Your life is a speck of sand in the great big ocean shore of humanity currently being beaten upon by the tidal wave of time and change. God is in the midst of shaking awake a whole generation of women who've had sleep dust sprinkled on them. *"It's time."* *"You can wake up now."* *"You've slept long enough."* *"It's time to reclaim your lives."*

It's not coincidental that Mary and Elizabeth became pregnant right about the same time. Everything was in God's timing. God knew that Mary would need a confidante, spiritual companion, and wise soul to reach out to. And God knew that Elizabeth would need a friend who would be happy that her prayers were answered, someone else familiar with God's mysterious timing. Each confirmed for the other that with God all things were possible, especially new beginnings. "Synchronicity" is the term the Swiss psychoanalyst Carl Jung used in describing what happens when inner readiness intersects with outer opportunities. It's the curious way in which a person's external reality suddenly clicks into alignment with what's taking place in her inner world.

You decide one day that the way to do something about the sluggish and tired feeling you carry around with you all the time is to take better care of yourself, which for you spells exercising and laying off eating all the fast foods. Cooking your own meals, which you used to enjoy doing immensely, would help you eat more nutritiously, you reason. But you haven't done any regular cooking in years and feel unsure where to begin. While at the mall the next day, browsing around for new sandals, you happen to spot an announcement outside the posh kitchenware store: "Three-Week Cooking Class on Preparing Nutritious Meals." Coincidence? An internal revelation synchronizes with an external invitation. Synchronicity is God's way of nudging us along in the direction of our healing and wholeness, while at the same time remaining anonymous.

Gardening is a hobby and passion of yours. Set you

loose in a yard with a few seeds and a trowel, and time is forgotten. Your front yard is the envy of everyone in the neighborhood because you have a knack for planting things that keep your yard awash in color and full of foliage all year long. One morning after shutting off the sprinkler before heading for work, you tell yourself for the umpteenth time that you'd trade in your dull work as a personnel officer at the bank any day for the chance to work in a garden all day long. Four months later a pink slip is on your desk. Terror strikes. Teary eyed and shaken all week, you can hardly get through those last days, anxious about how you're going to make it without a job. A week later, while working late in your garden one evening, praying and crying, your mind hardly on what you're doing, a neighbor stops by to ask a favor. Her daughter is getting married in a year and wants to have her wedding in her parents' backyard. Your neighbor is terrified because her yard is a mess. She offers to hire you to help her figure out what she can plant now in order to make her yard presentable for a wedding a year from now. Coincidence? I don't think so. The universe, at God's command, is waiting for us to be available to receive what we need.

Is it possible to miss opportunities that come our way? Of course it is. But it's also possible that the reason we miss them is because we're not ready from within and there's no one around us with the wisdom and experience to help identify for us what's going on in our lives. Some opportunities come around once in a lifetime, but some other opportunities come back around and meet us when we're ready. God repeatedly holds out to us the chance to start over, begin anew, go to the next level. God is not like those of us who give the people we love one, two, maybe three chances to choose and get it right. *Behold, I stand at the door and knock*, says the Holy One (Rev. 3:20). God knocks repeatedly.

Think about the moments when certain things fell apart or when other things came together in your life. Had you been in your mid-twenties instead of being in your late thirties when you discovered that your last boyfriend couldn't find it in himself to make a commitment to you, you may have lingered in the relationship longer, hoping, wishing, thinking something was wrong with you, trying to make him feel something he didn't feel. But you were older, you knew better, and you knew you deserved better. A few years back, you would have been too frightened to step out and start your own business, but after twenty years of making lots of money for someone else, you know you have what it takes to make money under your own logo. A decade ago you would not have picked up a book on spiritual readiness. But today you can't read enough about reinventing yourself. *It must be God.*

The point is that there were times when you were simply too drained or terrified to seize a new opportunity, no matter how good an opportunity it was. There were other times when you were too content with the way things were to contemplate a change of any kind. Only when you're ready from within do you notice the stimuli God sends to awaken you and to nourish you. Only when you're at that critical juncture when all systems within are at alert are you likely to embrace the teacher who comes along to introduce you to new ways of thinking and seeing the world. "When the teacher is ready, the student will come" is the way Eastern mystics describe this intersection of inner readiness and divine opportunity.

Had Mary's pregnancy proceeded normally—within the bonds of sexual intimacy with Joseph, her husband, and without God's miraculous intervention—she might have scoffed at the idea of dropping everything and visiting her cousin Elizabeth in the hill country. Had Elizabeth gotten pregnant earlier, when other women her age were having babies, she may have joined the women in the town in looking scornfully on Mary's claim that she was a virgin and pregnant. Answers to our prayers blow upon us all the time. There are seasons when we're simply not available emotionally, spiritually, psychologically, and even physically to recognize them and seize them as the gifts from God which they are. Unfortunately, it often takes a personal crisis to get us to be alert to the people who come into our path and the opportunities that open up. It shouldn't have to take a personal crisis, but often it does. We would all do well to pay particular attention to the people who come into our lives at critical junctures along our journey. They come to teach us important lessons—both positive and negative lessons. The strangers whose conversation on the subway doesn't easily vanish from your mind, the book on your sister's shelf that changed your life, the guest lecturer whose offhand remark unlocked a stubborn mystery, the long-lost classmate who finds you through the Internet, the client who compliments you for something you didn't know you'd done—these are not mere casual occurrences. *Pssssttt.* They are messengers from God.

By the time the angel Gabriel left Mary with the bittersweet news about the child she was carrying, Mary was anxious to visit Elizabeth. That someone else knew personally what it meant to experience an unlikely pregnancy emboldened Mary to risk her family's disapproval by taking off in the middle of her engagement for an unplanned trip to Judah. But Mary followed her instincts. She had to be certain. She had to see for herself. She needed a woman who could tell her that on the other side of the losses are gains to be had.

"*Even Elizabeth . . .*" the angel said.

Talk to other honest women. They will tell you that while it hurts to peel back the skin to find out what you're really made of, it's worth it. Despite all the tears, the screams, the yelps, the thrashing around that you and those around you go through after you've decided it's time for some changes, it's possible to come through it stronger and more true to yourself. Don't bother talking to the ones who are currently in the same stage of denial you were in a year ago. They can't tell themselves the truth yet. Completely bypass the sleepwalkers. They are still waiting for something or someone to come along to rescue them from having to take responsibility for their own happiness. But somewhere in your sphere of movement is "even Elizabeth." She is far enough along in her own metamorphosis to show you that it's never too late to find your place in the world. While you're at it, stop waiting for God to send some extraordinary, extraterrestrial, supernatural sign to confirm that you're on the right path. All you really have to do is look around at the women in your family, your church, your neighborhood, your sorority, on your job, ordinary women with extraordinary testimonies of where the mystery of God will take you when you surrender to it. Every woman has or will experience her own share of growing up and growing older. It's up to you to find other women and allow them to speak truth to you in your secret places.

It's as though I said yes to you, God, and the whole
universe opened up to me.
Everywhere I turn, someone is talking about change.
Nothing feels like a coincidence. Everything feels as
though it's been waiting for me
to open my eyes.
Why have I never noticed before?
And now that I do see,
I know that I can never un-see what I see, nor
un-know what I know.
I can't go back to the old woman.
I don't want to go back.
She doesn't live here anymore.
Even though I don't know who this woman is,
or what she will be when God is finished with her,
I do look forward to meeting her.

Overshadowed

"A side of her will never belong to you," the angel told Joseph the day he visited the Galilean carpenter and confirmed for him the divine nature of his fiancée's pregnancy. "She is your wife, but before she was your wife she was, and will always be, a daughter of the Divine One." What a jolt the angel's words must have given Joseph. What startling news to find out about someone you thought *belonged* to you. Your spouse. Your child. Your best friend. Your mother. Your sister. Your*self*. Forget what you've heard previously about the angel coming to reassure Joseph that Mary was still a virgin and that she wasn't pregnant by another man. (Matt. 1:19–25). No, no, no. The angel (and God) didn't care a thing about Joseph's wounded honor. Not really. Consider for a moment the angel warning Joseph, "Be careful how you treat her, because this woman is special." Matthew admits that it took an angel appearing to Joseph in a dream one morning as

Joseph tossed back and forth in bed trying to figure out a way to distance himself from Mary. Some men (and women) know it instinctively, some men (and women) have to be clued in about a woman's true worth. There are parts of the person you love dearly that you'll never be able to understand fully. That part belongs to God.

To be overshadowed by the Creator's holy presence, as Mary was, means in one sense that you can never completely belong to anyone, not even to yourself. Parts of you are unconquerable. Try as he may, try as you may, you will never be completely satisfied with human love. Something will always be missing. You will be forever searching for something more. The more is the sacred, a taste of the holy, the mystery of the divine. Alone with the Alone. Joseph can never love you enough to obliterate your need for God. (Nor will you ever be able to satisfy him so that he will not crave some quiet time for himself.) You will always yearn. Recall the psalmist's plaintive sigh, *As a deer thirsts for flowing streams, so pines my soul after thee, O God. My soul thirsts for the Living God . . .* (Ps. 42:1–2). The difference between the psalmist and many of us is that we are not sure what will satisfy our thirst. Love. Money. Children. Better job. Bigger house. Nicer car. Prestige. And we can't understand why none of these things satisfy us quite the way we thought once we get a taste of them. *Why after a scrumptious meal at such a fine restaurant am I still hungry?* you secretly wonder to yourself as you pull out your wallet to pay the bill. Maybe it was the company you keep. Perhaps it wasn't something about the food or the menu that left you still hungry. Perhaps it was the dull conversation around the table, or the failure of you and those around you to connect.

"How is this possible?" Mary asked the angel. His reply to her was, "The Holy Spirit will come upon you, and the power of the Most High will overshadow you." None of us knows for sure what all this means. But part of what it must mean is that something about you will always be a mystery. Something in you will always defy convention and definition. You cannot be possessed. To be created in the image and the likeness of God, as we all are, is to know what it means for the human and the divine parts of ourselves to be always in tension with each other. The human side always craves more: *If only I had that, if only I had more, if only I had what she has. . . .* The divine side always craves less: *Less is more, less is more, less is more.* Mary, like all of us, would spend the rest of her life trying to strike a balance between her need for human intimacy and her need for time with God and herself.

No one tells you this before you get married, but I will. A side of you will always be lonely, even in marriage, even as you're enfolded by the warm, tiny bodies of your children sleeping with you on one side of the bed and your husband's reassuring snore on the other side, even though your life is full of family, friends, and satisfying work. You will always suffer from bouts of loneliness. It comes from our being part human and part divine. Of course, "loneliness" is a dirty word in our modern vocabulary. It is poor taste to admit to feeling lonely. Only the flawed confess that they are lonely. We admonish parents to have more children so that the only child won't be lonely. (I can't tell you how many times as a mother of one child I've heard this one.) Spiritual pundits go to great lengths to convince us that we're not really lonely. They tidy up our feelings by telling us that we're not lonely. There's a difference between being lonely and being alone, they say. You can be alone without feeling lonely, they tell us. And they are correct, in part.

Being alone and being lonely should not be confused with one another. We all know what it feels like to be crowded in by the demands of others so much that we crave time alone, time to ourselves, time for private thoughts. Time alone gives us the chance to refuel and regroup so we may return to our schedules. But few of us who crave time alone want to live permanently alone and isolated from relationships. Loneliness, as we usually think of it, is feeling desolate and empty for lack of constant companionship. God, I believe, understands fully our need for companionship, intimacy, relationships, connectedness, and to be touched meaningfully by other human beings. Nowhere in Scripture does God confine a human being to permanent isolation. Even those in Scripture whose singleness or childlessness is traced back to God's doings are still allowed to enjoy the warmth and pleasures of being in a family and having friends. *[God] puts the solitary in families* is the way one psalmist puts it (Ps. 68:6). God's reassurances may be uttered to individuals, but they are always made on behalf of tribes, clans, families, relationships, and generations.

But there is a loneliness that is intrinsic to our humanity. No amount of love, friendships, and sexual encounters can extinguish it. Try as you may to fill that loneliness with more people, more stuff, more activity, more time away from your Self, the more you try, the more insistent it is. Stop it. No Joseph, no baby, no career can fill it. That's the place within us that God seeks to occupy. That's the loneliness designed to drive you to the edge of mystery. "As a deer thirsts for flowing streams, so pines my soul after thee, O God. My soul thirsts for the Living God . . ." (Ps. 42:1–2).

In our lonely places is where we encounter the Holy. Loneliness can be an invitation from God to draw closer to the flame. Loneliness is where you have opportunity to touch the source of your strength. In your loneliest moments, you come face-to-face with your truest self. "Make the loneliness go away," we say to God. "If I were married, I wouldn't be lonely." "With a child in my life, there wouldn't be time to be lonely." True and not true. If you were married, you would enjoy the companionship of a spouse, and it's true that as humans we are wired for companionship. It's also true that if you had a child, your child's needs would see to it that your schedule was full and exhausting, at least for the next eighteen years. But even with husband and child in tow, it's still possible, likely even, to find yourself irrationally seized by fits of longing for something you can't put your finger on. You find yourself asking yourself, *Is this all there is to my life? I'm blessed, but why can't I be satisfied?* Like Snow White's self-absorbed and tormented stepmother, who in one version of the story goes from one mirror to another mirror in the palace, seeking a better reflection of herself, the inner woman demands another mirror be brought in so that she can see her true Self.

Accept it: A side of you will never belong to your lover, your children, your friends, your family, or your colleagues. And when you risk parts of yourself to fulfill all their needs so that they may adore you forever, don't be hurt or surprised when after tossing you around, they gobble you up, without so much as a "Thank you," and demand more. That's what people do when they are given something they don't know the value of. Draw a line in yourself like the one you drew when you and your sister shared the same bedroom. This is your side of the room, and this is my side of the room. Okay, so you both discovered to your chagrin that it's impossible to keep the other completely out of your sacred territory. People misplace things all the time and wander into your territory because they suspect that you have what they are looking for, just like your sister was always traipsing over into your domain for her misplaced barrettes. But the line served its function. You and your sister were teaching each other about boundaries, about privacy, about having some space for yourself. *This is where you end, and I begin.* Your side of the room was where you could relax and be with your Self. This is the place (or time or space) within that belongs to no one other than God and yourself. And even if you look up and discover that you've inadvertently let Joseph or others cross the threshold and trespass into your sacred territory, don't be surprised if you find yourself one day screaming and yelling, unable to get out anything more articulate than "Get out!" If you feel like a madwoman on those occasions, you're not. Even if you temporarily look and sound like one. It will pass. The real madwoman is the one who has people stomping around in her sacred space, the space where she and God alone meet and commune, and no alarm inside her has sounded. She's out of touch with the divine within her.

No, that doesn't belong to me.
I'm sorry, but that doesn't involve me.
I'm not available to hear that today.
No, I am not doing anything today. But the nothing
I'm doing will be done by myself, for myself.
Yes, I am alone. And it's okay.
Yes, I am sitting here in the dark. And no,
I don't want company.
Excuse me, you can't occupy that place in
my life anymore.
Get out of here!
Give my self back!
Let go of me!
I love you, but I can live without you.
That woman doesn't live here anymore.
This space is now reserved for me.

Sex and Sleep
Dust

❦

Engagement between a woman and a man was serious business in Mary's times. Mary and Joseph's marriage was probably negotiated and arranged by their parents. The discussions between the two sets of parents was a very ceremonial affair in which the family of the husband-to-be would go to the home of the family of the bride-to-be, and there the young man's father would ask the young woman's father (or male legal guardian) for permission for his son to marry her. As evidence of the seriousness of it all, both families would spend the better part of the evening haggling out the details and the terms of the marriage. The young woman's family could tell the seriousness and earnestness of the request by the "bride's price" the husband-to-be's family was willing to pay for the girl. The girl's family in turn was expected to give their daughter a dowry commensurate with their status and honor in the community. The daughter's dowry would accompany the girl in marriage and become the common property of the bride and her husband.

It was customary for the whole community to wait anxiously throughout the evening for a sign that the negotiations had not broken off and that a party was still on the horizon. If the terms were acceptable, both families would emerge from the home full of smiles, hugs, pats on the back, all signs that the celebration could begin. There would be a feast, and from that moment on, the two young people were married, sort of. I say "sort of" because custom demanded that a yearlong engagement period ensue, in which the two young people did not live together but used the time to get to know each other and to get used to the idea of being wife and husband. They had a year to learn and study each other's ways, without sex weaving its magical powers to blind them to the things each would discover about the other. Although there was sure to be a big celebration after the year was over, there was a famously festive ceremony the evening the betrothal began. The thinking was that the lives of the two young people began the night the two families agreed to each other's terms. So important was this occasion that Jesus' own ministry reportedly began at a wedding ceremony. He rescued the host by replenishing the supply of wine on hand for the many guests who'd come to toast the new couple.

It goes without saying that the new wife was expected to remain chaste and devoted to her husband. If she slept with another man during this time, by law both were to be stoned to death (Deut. 22:24). The thought of a young bride making off with another man during that year's time, while her husband-to-be was trying to build a house for his new wife and himself and accumulate enough money to pay the final installment on the bride price, struck at the heart of male pride and honor. Abomination! During that year, Mary was supposed to be busy getting her dowry together and accumulating the odds and ends she would need to set up house with her new husband.

It was during this yearlong marriage-engagement period that the angel Gabriel visited Mary. You see, then, that lots of things were at stake in the news Mary carried in her womb the evening Gabriel left her. Three disasters were at hand: First, her family's honor was at stake if news got out that she had gotten herself pregnant by someone other than her husband. They would have to scrape up the portion of the bride price already doled out by the husband-to-be (which surely they'd spent within that year) and return it to the family of the husband-to-be. Second, her husband-to-be would be humiliated and dishonored, and any rash acts on his part to restore his honor would be tolerated and justified by the community. Third and finally, the very life of the bride-to-be was at stake. She deserved to be stoned to death. Imagine a girl, twelve to seventeen years old, shouldered with this kind of responsibility for a deed she did not invite upon herself. Mary could have said no. Who could blame her? Being a betrothed bride was serious business.

The purpose of the betrothal period was to give a bride and her husband time to know each other. Imagine a year of being able to enjoy blissful romance without sex complicating the relationship and without it forcing ripeness where there's only a tiny, immature sprout. It's a completely opposite way of thinking about love, courtship, and marriage from our own in this culture. The sexual revolution of the last forty years has resulted in our not knowing how to interact with the opposite sex anymore without testing their sexual prowess early on in the relationship. Sex, not shared values or good communication, has become the litmus test for two people's compatibility. Today, many argue that premarital intimacy is necessary because it's important to know if one's future mate has what it takes to satisfy you sexually before committing to him or her in marriage. One might say that ours is a time when people believe that having an orgasm in marriage is an inalienable right, whereas people once turned to religion for that heady, out-of-body experience of ecstasy and spiritual union with the Creator. We live during a time when sex is the new spirituality, in that we turn to sex to help us escape the profanity of everyday life. We rely upon quick and easy sex to fill our loneliness and to force a bond where there is none. This is absolutely backward from the way Mary's generation imagined it would be. Spending time with each other and taking the time to contemplate the idea of spending the rest of your lives together were virtues. The elders in the community trusted that the couple in time and with patience would learn how to satisfy each other sexually in the marriage relationship.

For as far back as the times when people worshiped both the masculine *and* feminine parts of God's divine being, celibacy was a virtue. With celibacy there's the possibility of one learning what it means to live a disciplined life. If Mary and Joseph had enough discipline to withhold themselves from sex during their one-year engagement, there was a chance they would be able to bring that same discipline into the marriage and respect the spiritual and bodily integrity of each other in the waxing and waning of marital love. Mystics living as celibates in cloistered communities have written time and again about the strength, clarity, and energy that can be had from harnessing one's sexual drive and pouring it into creative and lofty endeavors.

Mary's and Joseph's families understood well the powerful hold that sex has over the imagination, forcing a relationship where there was never meant to be one, forcing intimacy where there was only lust, twisting an innocent crush into a full-blown affair. Sex changes relationships. Once the two of you have sex, the relationship changes, and you never go back to the presexual innocence of the relationship. Sleep dust falls. Sleep dust blinds you into thinking that the communication is really great, that the two of you share similar values, that you're destined to be with each other—when it's only the groping, fondling, and heavy breathing that's exciting.

A Japanese journalist writing a story on American marriages, and comparing them to the arranged marriages that still took place in traditional parts of Japan, once remarked that "American marriages start off hot and end up cold, whereas Japanese marriages start off cold and end up hot."

With stories about sexual misconduct on the part of leaders constantly headlining the news, with television and popular music using increasingly sexually graphic imagery to get across their messages, with growing numbers of teens admitting to being sexually active by the age of sixteen despite the increasing threat to this age group of contracting the AIDS virus, talking to today's streetwise teens and enlightened adults about celibacy and sexual discipline sounds like lectures from the prehistoric ages. *What for? Why wait? Are you serious?* How do you explain to someone gripped by swings in their hormones that bodily fluid is not the only thing exchanged in the hot, torrid moment of sexual bliss? How do you get across to them that your whole history as both a human and spiritual being is being passed back and forth in that wild, passionate moment? Every female (or male) he has slept with before, and every male (or female) she has slept with before, come together in that one moment. You exchange pasts. You also put your futures at risk, all for someone you've known for only a month, a week, a night. You don't even know his family. Something is wrong, tragically wrong, when you're willing to exchange bodily fluids and serve up the most secret parts of yourself to someone whose only redeeming quality is that he drives a nice car and has bedroom eyes. As one anonymous writer so inelegantly but aptly wrote, "Don't let your body write a check that it will take a lifetime to cash."

In Mary and Joseph's day, people believed that a couple had a lifetime to explore each other sexually. First things first. Spend time getting to know each other. Learn how to communicate with each other. Observe each other. Watch him among his own people. See how he treats the women in his family. Don't confuse lust with love. Just because you fall in love doesn't mean you have to marry. In many cultures today it remains the custom for parents to arrange the marriages of their children, according to what they feel are the best interests of both families. Ancient people were fully aware of the intoxicating effects of love, as evidenced by these words in the most excellent book of love, Song of Songs.

> Place me like a seal over your heart,
> like a seal on your arm;

for love is as strong as death,
and jealousy as unyielding as the grave.
It burns like a blazing fire,
like a mighty flame.
Many waters cannot quench love;
rivers cannot wash it away.
If one were to give
all the wealth of his house for love,
it would be utterly scorned.

While I'm not sure I would want to live in a society where marriages were arranged, I do know after ten years of marriage that while it takes only a few minutes to make a vow, it takes a lifetime to try and figure out what you said in that moment of intoxicating romance. I also know now that when you marry a man, you marry his family, his family's history, his family's issues. The same applies when a man marries a woman. Your life, your flaws, your ambitions, and your history become intertwined with his life, his flaws, his ambitions, and his history. You would be wise to take the time to look a little longer before leaping. It helps to belong to a village of families, people modeling the give and take of intimacy, a supportive cast of families and friends who are willing to pitch in and encourage you through the rough spots. It sure helps to have couples like Elizabeth and Zechariah around to look to. Look to couples whose marriages have survived the wax and wane of lust, the false promises and raw passion of youth and the sober truth and shared experiences of marriage in the middle years, the joy of having a steady companion, the disappointments of loss, betrayal, and unanswered prayers, and the telltale signs of a faith that's been tried. You need people like Elizabeth and Zechariah pretty early in a marriage to remind young couples like Mary and Joseph that love is a vow and not a feeling.

But it's the toll unbridled sex takes on a woman's spirit that no one talks about enough. Here is where young girls seem most vulnerable to me and so unready for all that sexual awakening does to a woman. Young girls are not prepared to deal with the rewiring that sex does to the spirit. Spiritual energy too is exchanged in the sexual act. In that mysteriously powerful moment of two flesh becoming one, all of his or her hopes, dreams, and beliefs merge and become indistinguishable from one another. As long as a girl remains a virgin, her dreams are her own. But when she takes Joseph to her bed as a lover, his dreams become a part of her dreams. She will never belong to herself in quite the same way again. Decades of growing up and growing into a woman will have to be experienced to learn how to disentangle herself from the heavy sound of his dreams and his aspirations, and to become her own person again.

The writer of the Book of Genesis was particularly sensitive to the heavy burden the woman shouldered after enjoying her first taste of the apple: *And your de-*

sire shall be for your husband, and he shall rule over you (Gen. 3:16). Hmmmm. For years, commentators have bickered back and forth about what that particular statement means. I don't pretend to have the answer, but years of observing women twisting and contorting themselves in order to satisfy the men they love, locking large chunks of themselves away in dark places in order to be loved, pretending to feel things they don't feel and pretending to be women they weren't, have convinced me that our desire to please and the price some of us are willing to pay to be in a relationship are more than bad habits we've picked up.

What makes a woman go against everything she knows is right, sound, and rational for the illusion of romance? How do we help our daughters make better decisions about their bodies and their souls than those we made at the height of the sexual revolution? We grew up under the banner of free love, only to grow into our thirties, forties, and fifties and find out that there is no such thing as free love. Eventually the bill comes due—broken promises, mistaken love, false intimacy, lingering diseases, undisciplined passion, the fear of being alone and standing on your own. Somehow we must find a way to save our daughters from the spell of the sleep dust that descends gently upon the shoulders of women.

*I have given myself away to so many people that
I don't remember who has what part of me.
I have fallen in love so many times, I don't even
bother to get up anymore.
If this isn't love, what I'm offering him today,
then I must tell him that it will just have
to do until the real thing comes.
He will just have to wait. Because I have
to wait . . . until I know what it is that I'm feeling.
I didn't know before. But now I do.
And now before it's too late,
God, cleanse me from all the spirits clinging
to me that do not belong to me.
No wonder—
Teach me how to love my Self.
Teach me how to love without giving up large parts
of myself.
Show me what it looks like to love and be free
at the same time.
Until then,
I can wait.*

Here Comes the Bride

Perhaps, like me, you have seen otherwise savvy, sensible, intelligent women lose all their wits when the time comes to plan their wedding. I have known women who have spoken their minds all their lives, worked hard for every accomplishment, studied long and hard for their degrees and fought to be paid what was due them—independent-minded women—whose brains turned to mush at the chance to star in their own wedding.

Too bad we have little information about what actually took place at ancient marriage ceremonies. What little we know can only be inferred by piecing together information from various books. The central ritual of the ceremony itself appears to have been the symbolic bringing of the bride into the groom's house, on a makeshift carriage resembling a marriage bed (Song of Songs 3:6–11), followed by great rejoicing. The groom wore a garland on his head, evidently designed for him by his mother (Song of Songs 3:11); the bride was bedecked head to toe with jewels (Isa. 61:10) and wore her finest apparel, along with a veil (Gen. 29:23–35). A lengthy celebration followed with merrymaking, singing (Jer. 16:9), and a weeklong fete (Judg. 14:12). It was a grand ceremonial climax to a year of suppressed desire: looking but no touching, yearning but no fulfillment, fantasizing but no outlet.

    This ritual as it has been passed down in the West lets girls imagine themselves as princess for the day and is perhaps the only ritual where a female is the center of attention, where her every whim and fancy is to be fulfilled, where all planning for the enchanted hour revolves around making her look beautiful, breathtaking, and desirable. Talk about a ceremony that perpetuates the image of the bride as the eternal daughter that must be forever taken care of, the beautiful but helpless daughter, the innocent but demanding female!

    As girls we were all bombarded from a very young age with reams and reels of images of the waiflike young woman dressed from head to toe in a white gown symbolizing her purity, with train and veil as part of her armor against the lecherous stares of the world, stepping amidst flower petals to signal her innocence, surrounded by giggly attendants who await her whim. Her entrance is the peak of the ceremony. At the end of her ceremonial walk into the room awaits her

Prince Charming, who stands ready to kiss her and awaken her to a new life of matrimony. Movies, magazines, and Web sites capture the imagination of girls and teach them to giddily anticipate the day when they get to produce, direct, and star in a ceremony given in their honor. I remember cutting classes in college, along with the other girls in my dorm, to catch Laura and Luke's royal wedding on *General Hospital.* I was transfixed. What was I thinking about?

"A girl's wedding day" is the day a woman gets to project and idealize herself as the most innocent of girls. Talk to some women years after the wedding when the reality of marriage has set in, and you may be surprised at what you hear. "At least I got to have the wedding I always wanted," says one woman I know, "even if the marriage started unraveling as I knew it would after only three months." For some women, marriage is anticlimactic in comparison to being able to star in a wedding. I think back with a chuckle to my own wedding ten years ago, recalling how I thought I had expunged from my ceremony what I believed were the most obnoxious elements of traditional weddings (e.g., bridesmaid, flower girl, escort by father, vows promising obedience, pronouncements that we were now "man and wife"). I outwitted patriarchy, or so I thought, by writing my vows, by having a husband-and-wife clergy couple perform the ceremony, by walking unescorted down the aisle, and by instructing the

minister to say at the end, "Whom God has joined together, let no man *or woman* put asunder." So why did
it never dawn on me to consider a color other than
white or ivory (I can't recall exactly which it was now)
for my African-inspired dress?

Wedding ceremonies are certainly about sealing the
love between a woman and a man, but there remains
an unmistakable trace of Old World thinking behind
some of its traditions that leaves one to suspect that the
ceremony is also about witnessing the bargain struck
between the father of the bride and the husband-to-be.
The helpless daughter grows up believing that auton-
omy and independence are unbecoming in a woman
and that the way to please men is to remain an eternal
girl and to put yourself in situations where men must
constantly come to your rescue. There are undeniable
advantages to being the eternal girl. To be able to rely
upon someone you perceive as stronger than you to
take care of you, to be admired by him as his "baby
cakes" for your agreeableness, adaptability, and gentle
demeanor. To be able to believe you were rescued and
carted off by a charming prince into his make-believe
kingdom is intoxicating for many, many women. Indeed, what it means for a woman to be beautiful in this
culture is tied to images of her as thin, delicate, frail,
waiflike, young, and dollish looking. A man is expected to marry a woman who has a smaller frame, is
shorter, younger, weaker, less educated, earns less

money (if any at all), and who defers to his naturally better judgment when the time comes to make a decision. Conversely, a woman is expected to marry a man with a broader build, someone taller, older, stronger, more educated, who earns more money and who is fearless to do what he must to protect her, even from herself.

Our society devotes a lot of thought, energy, and expense to keeping women girls and keeping us looking and acting as though we're helpless. Whole industries are given over to making sure we are dissatisfied with the way we look and preoccupied with disfiguring our bodies in ways that make them unrecognizable even to us. Both the cosmetics industry and the dieting industry depend on women becoming fearful and anxious about growing older. All the emphasis is on the outer woman. Weddings cast all attention on the outer woman, when the health of a marriage in the long run will depend in greater part on the interior, spiritual knitting together of the two people's lives.

But what makes a woman turn off the television, or flip past the magazine ads, and take responsibility for resisting those currents in the culture that keep her more preoccupied with the exterior than the interior woman? What makes her find the courage to look at the parts of her life that have been retarding her growth, and when is she most likely to shore up the resolve to begin making changes in her life? It is most likely to happen, if it ever does, at the moment when she stares at the face in the mirror and confronts the very real possibility that more years are perhaps behind her than there are ahead of her. You suddenly realize that while you can never know how and when you're going to die, you may as well do what you can now to decide how you're going to live out the years you have remaining.

All those years waiting to be loved the way we'd seen on television, waiting to be chosen, waiting to be noticed, waiting to be asked. All those years waiting. Never once did we question the images we saw. We didn't know that it was all a lie: the fairy-tale weddings, the soap opera romance, the smiling waiflike blonde in the advertisement. We didn't think to question the script handed to us. We thought something was wrong with us, our lives, and our bodies.

"When Sleeping Beauty wakes up," writes the poet Maxine Kumin, "she is almost fifty years old." Before that time she's still waiting to be rescued. Waiting for someone to come along, or waiting for passion to awaken her, waiting for something to happen that will save her from having to make decisions about the course of her life. But by the time a woman turns fifty, say the experts, she is likely to have seen through the myths. Of course, it doesn't have to take that long. You can begin today, right now, at this moment. Wake up. It's time. Being twenty-something or forty-something is just as good a time as any to start giving as much attention to the inner woman as to the outer woman. These are ripe years for waking up and discovering the true you.

Of course, some women claim not to have any regrets about a forgotten self. They deny ever dreaming of becoming anyone other than who they are right now or doing anything other than what they are doing at the moment. They are the lucky ones, perhaps. Or they are the ones who find self-scrutiny much too threatening. It's simpler to leave well enough alone. It's safer to go back to sleep, even though you can never un-see the parts of your life you've already seen.

Part of awakening, however, involves coming face-to-face with a neglected side of yourself, a side you've kept hidden for all these years, which now insists upon being taken seriously. When you were younger, before you got hooked on soap operas, you wanted to travel and see far-off places, but had to put that on the back burner once the babies started coming. And now that the babies are grown and having babies of their own, you've run out of excuses. Why not now?

Dreaming of walking down a long aisle in a glamorous wedding gown, with a tall, dark, and handsome prince standing at the altar awaiting you, may be part of your fantasy. But that's only one fantasy that you have, hopefully. How about your other dreams and fantasies? How about the other things you longed to do that weren't tied to whether he came along, or whether he was Mr. Right, or whether he wanted to do what you wanted him to do? What are you doing about those dreams? Those are *your* dreams. Somewhere in them lies the key to the authentic you. Invest yourself there.

You dreamed of one day recording all those wild and crazy family stories that get passed down every year at your family reunions and publishing them for everyone, but you've never gotten it off the ground what with a full-time job and family. But now the kids are older and have their own activities, and a blank computer screen sits off in a corner of the kitchen. So, what's keeping you? You're thirty-something now, successful, financially comfortable, respected in your profession, and beginning to feel, well, restless. Lately the dream of picking up your paintbrush again and buying art paper has resurfaced. Where did these strange urges come from? They're the neglected, forgotten parts of ourselves that peep up in our consciousness, demanding our attention, reminding us that there's more to being a woman, being alive, being you than even you know. Only then are you likely to begin the slow, painful process of peeling off the mask you wore eagerly when you were a girl and peering curiously at the face of the woman you have kept hidden all these years.

A popular rabbinical puts the matter this way: When you die and go to Heaven and meet your Maker, your Maker is not going to ask, "Why didn't you discover the cure for such and such? Why didn't you become a leader? Why weren't you successful? Why didn't you do more? Why weren't you the best?" The only question the Maker will ask you in that precious moment is "Why didn't you become you?"

Create in me, O Lord, a new picture for myself.
Hold up the mirror that reflects back to me the God
within me,
the good in me, the whole in me, the love in me, the
laughter in me,
the power within me.
Let me see me, so I can be the me you created
me to be.
Renew my self-image.
Show me reflections that say,
I am not helpless. I am not weak. I am not powerless.
I am not a victim.

I am no longer asleep,
I am fully conscious.
And now that I am awake
I've got plans for me.

My Mother, My Self

❦

*H*ave you ever noticed how often the female protagonists in popular children's fairy tales are motherless girls? I have. Beautifully illustrated copies of "Cinderella," "Rumpelstiltskin," "Rapunzel," "Sleeping Beauty," and "Snow White" line my daughter's bookshelf, and on those occasions when I've read one of them to her at night we're both unsatisfied midway through the book. I can never come up with anything satisfying in response to her questions, "Where was her mother?" or "What did her mother say?" or "What did her mother do when that happened to the daughter?" The thought of a mother leaving her daughter to face a danger or a tension-filled challenge alone is unimaginable to my daughter's young mind. It's unimaginable to me too. But I'm the adult, and I know it's not as simple as that: Danger is inherent to life. Mothers can't always be there to protect their children as much as they'd like to; mothers die, leave, emotionally unravel, or sometimes are too distracted with their own worries to come to their daughters' defense, leaving their daughters to grow up quicker than they would otherwise. And, of course, most classic fairy tales were written or recorded by men, and as such reflect male interests. It seems that mothers are dispensable when men are telling stories about daughters. But my daughter's persistent questions about the whereabouts of the mothers of Cinderella, Rapunzel, Sleeping Beauty, and Snow White does make me wonder.

It makes me wonder about Mary's mother. Why did Mary seek our her older cousin Elizabeth rather than her own mother? Who was Mary's mother? Why do the mothers of all the interesting women in literature die in childbirth or lose influence over their daughters after childbirth?

I have a married friend who couldn't bring herself to tell her mother that she was pregnant. Each time she spoke with her mother on the phone, the words kept getting stuck in her throat. My friend's husband finally had to tell his mother-in-law that her daughter was pregnant. It seems that his wife couldn't bring herself to admit to her mother that she'd been having sex (with her own husband!). She and her mother had never talked about sex before beyond her mother's routine admonishment during her teenage years: "Don't you dare let me hear about you doing it" or "Nice girls don't do it." "It" pretty much summarizes what so many of our mothers said about sex. Despite masquerading as modern women, most of us, like my girl-friend, absorbed our mothers' attitudes about sex and pregnancy. Nothing tries the mother-daughter bond more, nothing discloses more about a mother-daughter relationship, than when the time comes to talk about sex and pregnancy. Can you remember your mother's discussions with you about sex? Who did most of the talking? What was your reaction when the topic came up? What was her response when you told her you were pregnant? How much different was the conversation you had with your daughter about sex and pregnancy? I try to talk with my eight-year-old daughter about sex and babies, and she rolls her eyes and mutters, "Oh, Mommy, I know this already. We don't have to talk about that."

Mary chose her older cousin over her mother to discuss what pregnancy was like. Perhaps Mary's own mother was dead. Perhaps Mary knew that her mother would have been skeptical about her story of being a pregnant virgin. Perhaps Mary simply couldn't bring herself to talk with her mother about sex and having babies. After all, nothing shoves you out of daughterhood and into womanhood like motherhood. I'm inclined to believe, however, that Mary's mother was neither dead nor unapproachable at the time Mary found out she was pregnant. What if she was simply a woman who had been wise enough to bless her daughter with a village of women to whom her daughter could turn when talking to one's mother seemed out of the question?

Sometimes the most precious gift a mother can give her daughter is to surround her with women she can confide in about subjects the daughter feels unprepared to broach with her mother. Every mother's daughter needs a coterie of women friends—aunts, play-aunts, godmothers, Big Mamas, Ma' Dears—to serve as role models, confidantes, and prayer warriors to help usher a girl from daughterhood to womanhood. The proverb "It takes a village to raise a child" can be adapted here as "It takes a village of women to raise a woman-child." Without a village of women acting as confidantes, prayer warriors, and guardian angels (to both mother and daughter), a mother can emotionally collapse from the weight of feeling overburdened by the constant demands made on her by her children. A daughter can remain the "eternal daughter" for lack of maternal intervention when she slips into passive, self-defeating behavior.

I'm grateful to my own mother that she modeled for me the importance of being surrounded by women friends. We moved around a lot when I was growing up, but whenever we moved, my mother always made friends with women in the neighborhood. She refused to allow my father to keep her isolated from other women as he would have preferred. My mother's single or childless girlfriends were, from my vantage point, the best of my mother's friends. They always had time for me and were never uptight talking to me about the things that made my mother cringe. I'm grateful that my mother never resented the time I spent at the homes of her childless girlfriends. She probably understood my need to talk to someone who didn't love me in that way that mothers love. I had to have a daughter of my own to forgive my mother for loving me that way. It's the kind of love that makes your heart drop to the floor at the first inkling that your child might be in trouble. You don't hear, you react. You don't understand, you're too busy rescuing. I needed an objective ear, and she trusted her friends to steer me right. It wasn't until much later that I figured out that despite the promises I extracted from them not to tell my mother what we talked about, her friends were wise souls. They knew when and what my mother needed to know. And they knew how to nudge me into talking to my mother about subjects they felt she needed to know, and how to help me not judge my mother so harshly for being imperfect.

The truth is, there are no perfect mothers. Perfect mothers exist only in myths. In real life, mothers make mistakes, they bumble their way through, learning as they go. They go back and forth between moments of feeling frustrated and overwhelmed by the constant demands of children and moments of profound love and elation at the mere sight of their children nearby. While some women may find certain aspects of care-giving instinctive, in truth the vast majority of caring for children must be learned and has to be passed down from one mother to the next. No one talks about this, of course. You sit at home alone for weeks with a new-born, berating yourself that here you are a mother and you don't know a thing about what to do with a crying baby, a fretful baby, a screaming baby, a baby that won't sleep. And you're ashamed to tell anyone. You look up one day and find yourself staring into the angry eyes of a daughter whose needs outstrip your ability to respond.

Both mother and child benefit when a village of extra hands and wise souls are available to share the parenting load. One woman may bear a child, but she depends upon the whole community to help her give life to that child. Mary turned to Elizabeth not because her mother was an ineffective mother. She turned to Elizabeth because she needed at the time the counsel of a woman who could listen to her, pregnant woman to pregnant woman, and not pregnant teenage daugh-ter to disappointed mother of a pregnant teenage daughter.

Remember when you were a teenager? Remember how difficult it was to talk to your mother about sex, boyfriends, your first crush, your first kiss? Distancing is an inevitable part of the parent-child dynamic. Part of growing up and developing into young adulthood involves distancing yourself from your parents. It's hard to do this if the teenager sympathizes too much with the pain and problems of those who nurture them. It's hard to do it when your teenager thinks you are a goddess. To separate and become their own person, they must see you as old-fashioned and pudding-headed. I'm sure you remember back to this time in your life well. I thought my parents were relics from the Stone Age. It helped to have aunts, older cousins, godmothers, grandmothers, wise girlfriends on hand to put my mother and her strange ways in perspective.

We've all learned by now that our daughters need the counsel of other mother figures in their lives to help them see their mothers as women first and not mothers only. Mary was blessed because she probably had her mother's permission and blessing to have other maternal figures around, Elizabeth being one, watching over her as she matured into womanhood. If you're a parent, the best gift you can give your child is to give them permission to talk with those you trust. If you're a woman with no daughters of your own, the greatest gift you can receive is the opportunity to be there for a girl as she looks around for role models, and when she needs a steady hand to help her cross the threshold from girlhood to womanhood.

Some mothers give birth physically. Some mothers give birth from the heart. Elizabeth was childless for many years. But from Mary's response to the news that the older woman too was pregnant, it's apparent that Elizabeth knew how to be a mothering presence in a young girl's life. If you don't have a child, you, like Elizabeth, can still lavish maternal affection upon some girl or boy. If you have nieces or nephews, spoil them with your time and attention, as much as with your gifts. If you don't have nieces or nephews, help your girlfriend out by taking her children off her hands sometimes, spend time with a youth in your church or in your apartment complex, or adopt a student at one of the local inner-city schools. Lavish them with attention by being available to listen without judgment to their questions, their troubles, and their triumphs. Who knows? Maybe you can intervene at just the right time and be God's gift to an overwrought and depleted parent who is at her wit's end with her daughter. As godmother, big sister, or play aunt, your task can be to help build a bridge of communication between an estranged mother and her daughter.

It is said that you are a Mother to the Motherless.
Suckle me with your breasts of comfort.
Soothe me with your loving embrace.
Teach me how to walk on my own.

Show me how to mother without wounding.
Show me how to receive mothering from others without
judgment and without embarrassment.
Thank you for the mother who brought me to life.
Show me how to forgive her for not living up to my
idea of what she should have been like.
Thank you for the woman she wanted to be.
May those who look up to me for mothering be more
forgiving than I was with my mother.

Shedding the Eternal Girl

$\mathcal{W}$ ithout a watchful mother figure to direct her and protect her, each girl in the fairy tales on my daughter's bookshelf is relegated to live out a period of time as a passive, wounded, helpless "eternal girl."

In each fairy tale the daughter suffers because of some avarice or ineptitude on the part of her father. In each the mother of the daughter is absent or silenced. The daughter is rendered helpless and infantile by the circumstances that have befallen her. "Puella" ("the eternal daughter") is the term therapists use to describe the woman frozen in time, playing the role of the poor "sweet young thing." Sweet, compliant, vulnerable, adaptable, and submissive, she remains fixed in a girlish level of development. The suffering of the "eternal girl" in many classic fairy tales is only relieved when a dashing prince comes along. The prince rescues her from her father's ineptitude and the devil's torture and takes her away to his palace, where she lives out the rest of her days in grateful obedience to him. How many women have resigned themselves to living in insufferable conditions, giving up their independence, settling for a passive, dependent life, in exchange for the promise of the safety and security of marriage? How often do we long to be delivered from ordinary life and transported to the fairy-tale life of eternal romance? Years later, most of these women feel they have been betrayed. They wake up one morning and discover that they are thirty, forty, fifty, sixty, and beyond, playing the pitiful part that no longer suits them, namely the sweet young (married) thing.

If you're still a sweet young thing, enjoy it. But you'd be wise to use this time developing your mind, exploring your spiritual side, spending time with God. Though not impossible, it's hard trying to create an inner sacred landscape after years of leaving that part of yourself fallow and undeveloped. When reality sets in at fifty, it helps to already be "on speaking terms with God," as the old women in my mother's church would say. If you're past the season of being anyone's trophy, prize, or sweet young thing, be grateful. You can now devote that energy to being a mellow, mature woman, alive, confident, fearless, a wise virgin.

All the fathers in the fairy tales leave their daughters to fend for themselves. Since Cinderella's father allows himself to be dominated by an insanely wicked second wife who condemns her stepdaughter Cinderella to live in rags and be a handmaiden to her own two equally wicked daughters, we can only assume that Cinderella's biological mother is dead. Similarly, Snow White falls victim to the murderously jealous fits of her stepmother. She eventually has to flee her father's palace and find safety in a cottage of dwarfs. We are left to assume that Snow White's biological mother is dead and unable to rescue her daughter from the wicked stepmother. In "Rumpelstiltskin," there is no mention of a mother or stepmother figure, only a father who brags to the king about his daughter's ability to spin straw into gold. The king forces the girl's father to hand his daughter over to him and shuts her away in a room by herself. There she strikes a bargain with the devil to teach her how to spin straw into gold in exchange for her firstborn child. Of the five stories, biological mothers appear in "Rapunzel," and "Sleeping Beauty," but only in the beginning, as barren women who pine away for a child. Once their wish is granted and their daughters are born, the mothers recede in the background and do not speak again. The inference in each story is the same: Motherless or mother-silenced daughters are vulnerable, weak, naive, servile, and unable to protect themselves.

To Mary's credit, she did not wait around for Elizabeth to come to her. Mary took the initiative to seek out her cousin for advice and reassurance. To raise a son with the mission of Jesus, Mary would need a template to use to transform herself from the young, naive, virginal girl to an astute, discerning, prayerful woman. She needed to be able to talk to other women who knew what it was to evolve and metamorphose, transform from being someone's sweet young thing to being an open, loving, but independent woman who belongs to herself.

I've always found it interesting that the Greek word for "soul" is *psyche*, and that both are often imagined and depicted as a butterfly. Both the soul and the butterfly undergo metamorphosis. Both change over a period of time. Unfortunately, the butterfly has one chance to get it right. The human soul, however, undergoes a hundred little metamorphoses in one's lifetime, each one more intense than the last, each designed to help you shed the fairy-tale layers of yourself you've outgrown, each one transforming you into a more authentic You. You've outgrown the days when it was enough to be a sweet young thing. Even if you're still young enough to be one. Spiritually, you've outgrown that stage in your life. God is calling you to a deeper life. It's not enough to be seductive, charming, and girlish. It's time to leave the cocoon and become a woman. At last, an angel, a voice within, comes along one day out of the blue, making impossible promises and making impossible demands, saying, in essence, "It's your time." Of course, it helps to have a circle of women standing by to witness and to celebrate the new you you've become in your rites of passage.

∞

I am a woman now, no longer a girl.
A daughter and at the same time a woman.
I have learned to speak up and speak out,
and to let my voice be heard in the forest.
It is time for me to take my place in the circle
of womanhood,
and claim my title as survivor, warrior, grown one,
eagle, mother earth.
I am entitled to the gray hair on my head.
I have earned the bags under my eyes.
I have won the right to the scar across my belly.
I have been to Hell and back, and God accompanied
me throughout the journey.
My days of being a sweet young thing are over.
I prefer being woman.

Midwives

List some of the ways in which friends have supported you through the years. Come on now, surely you don't mean to say that you've gotten to where you are without the help of anyone. No one put in a good word for you? Has no one patiently held the phone and listened to you rant or rave about some insanity taking place in your life? Has none of your friends ever offered to pray with you about a particular matter? Do you recall the name of the person who first introduced you to the church where you now belong?

Now list some ways you have supported your friends through the years. Don't be modest about the compassion you've tried to extend to others over the years. Don't tell yourself, *It was nothing.* To list your acts of compassion and sisterhood toward others is not bragging. It's to remind yourself that you've not always been on the receiving end of things, you're not just a taker. There have been seasons when you've been in a position to give support and seasons when you've had to step back and learn how to receive support.

Following in Mary's footsteps means following her example of bringing support to her friend Elizabeth as much as standing in need of support. When you support someone, you understand that your role is part of a larger process; you are not the solution. God, who is better equipped to know exactly what is needed, is at work in us, administering encouragement, support, kindness, and healing to those in need. Your task is to try to help your friend find strength in God. Your task is not to try to make everything right for her again. Knowing where you end and God begins frees you to let God use your service to draw to God those who stand in need of the Holy One.

Sometimes we let competition between us keep us from each other. Competition among women is a given in any society that values men over women and teaches women that they're incomplete without a man, any man. In such a society, women compete for the attention of men. Women view other women as their natural enemies and lose their connection to the women who nurtured them and served as guardian angels to them in their childhood. But at some point in our lives, usually when we're reeling from heartbreak, we find ourselves scrambling to find a sympathetic woman to lean on (e.g., a therapist, minister, or friend). If we're not careful, we can use these women as mere fill-in companions until we find new (male) lovers for ourselves. Most of us, however, eventually long for deep, abiding connections to other women. We miss the feminine in our lives. We miss having a circle of women, much like the one that nurtured us when we were still girls, to whom we can turn for comfort and friendship. We miss the gentle give and take of women's support networks: I'll comb your hair and you comb mine. I borrow your dress, you borrow my tennis shoes. We stay away from each other so long that we almost forget how to reach out and reconnect with each other. We almost forget how to ask for help and how to reach out and offer help to others.

We sometimes let our fears keep us from offering support to others and receiving support when it's offered to us. The fear of appearing pushy, meddling, or nosy keeps us from reaching out to others, and fear of seeming weak, dumb, or incapable of taking care of ourselves make us keep to ourselves and not ask for help. Mary could have chosen not to seek out Elizabeth, to remain in Nazareth and muddle through trying to persuade Joseph, her family, and all of Nazareth of her innocence. But she didn't. She found the courage to find Elizabeth, who lived miles away in the hills of Jerusalem.

In what has to be one of the most reassuring gestures in all of Scripture, the angel comforted Mary by assuring her that she was not alone in her journey.

Even her childless cousin Elizabeth was pregnant and already in her sixth month, despite her age. In other words, the God who can open the wombs of the barren is the same God who causes life to spring from the womb by divine fate. No matter how disturbing the news, no matter how calamitous the new beginning, God does not leave you alone to fit your life back together. Someone else has gone through or is going through what you're experiencing. You are not the first to have your plans dashed to the ground. You are not the first to wake up one morning to find your soul on the spin cycle. You are not the first to start over. You are not the only virgin in the world. Others know what it is to face an unknown future, and what it takes to reach deep within themselves to touch their inner wholeness. There are others further along in learning how to make a new life up as they go. Partner with other people, other pregnant virgins, those who have gone through or are now going through a similar dismantling of the old and awakening of the new and find ways to build support relationships with them.

To her credit, Elizabeth welcomed Mary in when she arrived. She could have slammed the door in her face. But she didn't. She opened her heart and home to Mary for those three months. She needed the young woman's support and presence as much as Mary needed her. According to the Scriptures, Elizabeth stayed secluded from the public for five months after discovering that she was pregnant. Elizabeth knew what her neighbors were saying. She knew she was the laughingstock of the town. She whose breasts were supposed to be too old to stir her husband's loins would have a baby sucking at her chest soon. What a joke! Though proud and elated that God had taken away the shame of her barrenness, still Elizabeth was not up to facing the stares, giggles, and pointing she would have to endure every day as she made her way to the well or to the market. Besides, she didn't want to risk miscarrying by overexerting herself. She needed time to adjust to being pregnant, and five months in seclusion would give those around her time to adjust as well. News of Mary's visit touched Elizabeth deeply. To the older woman, Mary was a sight for sore eyes. Elizabeth needed someone to talk to. It didn't matter that Mary was younger than she was. It wasn't until she beheld her cousin's face that Elizabeth knew how much she would probably need someone young and strong to help her in the weeks and months ahead.

Never underestimate the healing power of acts of friendship, support, and kindness. One loving word can lift a friend out of the depths of depression. One smile and "Good morning" can make someone feel loved. An offer to stay behind and wait with a visitor to your church whose car won't start and is waiting for a tow truck can make a difference in her life. Picking up a friend's daughter after school and chauffeuring her to gymnastics and piano practice, listening to her day, helping her with her homework, giving her dinner, and then depositing her safely back home can make both mom and daughter feel as though they've been touched by an angel that day. Ask God to reveal to you what person needs your ministry of support. You can't be available to everyone, nor can you be all things to all people. But you can ask God to show you how to love the people God directs to you, in the way they need to be loved, not the way you want to show love.

I am not the only one.
I am not alone.
I am not the only one pregnant.
Other women are changing before their
own eyes as well.
Other women are in the throes of
reinventing themselves.
Other women too need a helping hand.
Show them to me, God, so I won't wallow in self-pity
or think more of myself than I should.
Show me your face through a woman's face.
Let me hear your voice when my friend embraces me
saying, "Girl, where have you been? I've missed you."

Showing

Elizabeth was far enough along in her pregnancy to be physically showing by the time Mary arrived at her doorstep. She had been in seclusion for five months. That was enough time for her to adjust to her new life and to begin showing evidence of her changed state. After five months in seclusion and silence—her husband, Zechariah, had been struck temporarily mute by the angel because of his initial refusal to believe— imagine how glad Elizabeth was to have Mary to talk to when the younger woman arrived. By the time Mary came, Elizabeth was six months pregnant and strong enough to face the stares and giggles of those around her. The best friendships are the ones that encourage full personhood in each other. We know next to nothing about what the two women said or did those three months while they were together. The writer doesn't bother to say. We can only imagine. It was the last trimester of Elizabeth's pregnancy and the first trimester of Mary's. Mary found a new and different woman when she arrived at Elizabeth's doorstep, and Elizabeth found a girl faced with the awesome task of having to grow into womanhood in a few short months when she looked on the younger woman's face.

Sixth months into her pregnancy, Elizabeth was "showing" by the time Mary reached her. God directed Mary to a woman with evidence of being chosen and favored by God. God knew what kind of friend Mary needed. Trust God to bring the kind of friends that you need into your life. Trust God to bring along the friends you already have, if that is God's will. Don't underestimate God's ability to know which friends you need through the different phases of your becoming, and which ones your tender moments of unfurling can do without. God directed Mary to a woman with proof that God was using her in an extraordinary manner. Elizabeth wasn't likely to begrudge Mary her blessing when Elizabeth could point to proof of her own that God was using her. Mary needed someone who knew what it meant to have their life turned upside down by an act of God, someone who knew that even positive blessings can take some getting used to. She needed someone who understood that with some blessings the losses outnumber the gains in the beginning. But that's only what it feels like. See the change through to the end and your vision will become clearer. There are some necessary losses, but there are bound to be some very special gains as well.

Your courage to face the truth of your life will either propel your friends to find the courage to face the truth of their own lives, or it will make them turn away in fear and horror at the thought of stepping out onto the edge of mystery without a parachute. You have to be prepared for your friends' reactions when you start changing and becoming your own person. Some family and friends will stand by, cheering you on with prayers, patiently listening, and nodding knowingly at all the appropriate places. On the other hand, while you're as surprised as anyone else at what's happening in you, it can be even more difficult for others around you to accept what God is doing in you. After all, you've been eager to please for as long as they've known you. Sometimes people are happy that God is using you, but they resent the fact that that makes you no longer available to them. Others are downright hostile to the You you're becoming and will do everything they can to talk you out of unfurling your butterfly wings and growing. You have to be ready for the different kinds of reactions you will get. A change in someone who has lived her life trying to please others shakes up the safe, comfortable, familiar order of things. But once you start unfurling your wings, don't let others pressure or talk you back into the cocoon that once imprisoned you. Give people time to adjust, recognize their subtle (and not so subtle) efforts to obstruct or prevent your growth, listen patiently to their fears, reassure them, pray that God grant them a taste of mystery themselves, and then go on quietly becoming your new self.

"Are you showing?
How far along are you?
What's it like for you?
Show me your stretch marks, and I'll show you mine."
Isn't this just like God to bring us together?
God, teach me how to be a friend. Teach me how
to be friendly.
Teach me how to be genuinely happy for
another's blessings.
You don't have a limited number of blessings to
dole out to your children.
I am grateful that I lived long enough to know that
we can all be showing at the same time.

"But [She] Had No Children"

Stories in Scripture describing a male-dominated world where fertility in women was important to a man's honor and the survival of his clan make one pause and think about the thousands of women of childbearing age reading *Showing Mary* who have never given birth to a child and perhaps never will. A 1994 *New York Times*/CBS poll of American teenagers revealed that only 57 percent of teenage girls considered it very likely that they would have children. Historically, 3 to 30 percent of all women worldwide have not borne children. Also in 1994, close to 18 percent of American women were still childless by age forty. We are living in a time in history when never have so many Americans, whether by chance or by choice, known childlessness. The reasons that more and more women are childless are numerous, many of the reasons having to do with the unavailability of marriageable men. Reading the story of Mary and Elizabeth, you can't help asking yourself whether it's possible to live a happy, balanced, productive, full life as a woman and never give birth to a child. Of course it is, even though so many of the stories of women in the Bible center around women's experiences with pregnancy, childbirth, and motherhood. Clearly we are supposed to rejoice with barren women in Scripture like Elizabeth, Hannah, Sarah, and Rachel, who eventually come to experience the richness of motherhood as a result of God's intervention. But not every woman suffering from infertility will experience Elizabeth's miraculous good fortune.

Fortunately, rearing children is not the only way for a woman to enhance her personal growth. After all, people have babies for lots of reasons, and some of the reasons have little to do with the desire to nurture another life. Some people have children because they are lonely, others because of family and social pressure, still others are driven by baser motives that have much to do with competition, entitlement, and self-perpetuation. Women have had children for centuries, and many failed to take advantage of the opportunity for personal growth that maternity offered. It is possible to be a mother and remain a broken, narrow, shallow human being. In short, maternity is no guarantee of maturity. In Mary and Elizabeth's lifetime, motherhood was the epitome of the female experience. Whatever security, rewards, lessons, or spiritual growth a woman enjoyed was tied to her experiences of being a mother, a wife, a daughter, a daughter-in-law, a mother-in-law, or a grandmother. And as special and fulfilling as those roles were back then, and continue to be even now, there have always been women pressing for expanded possibilities for women. There have always been those of us who've wondered, to ourselves or out loud, whether God cared that some of us might not be mothers, wives, or grandmothers and were too old to be anyone's daughter.

If child rearing is the sole way for women to grow spiritually and emotionally, then what does one say to the large number of women who have put off getting pregnant until they find the right marriage partner? Will society applaud their choice or blast and accuse them of being choosy and uppity? The easiest thing would be to try to force women into compulsory marriages and compulsory pregnancies by reminding them that if they don't jump at the first chance that comes their way, there's a good chance that they will be past childbearing age before they happen upon partners they want to settle down with permanently. The harder thing to do would be to face up to the fact that in light of all the external pressure to become desperate and to cave in, it takes inner courage and a lot of self-esteem for a woman to decide to hold off from marrying and having babies until she's found that special someone.

And what about the others, that other group that's rarely talked about in Christian circles—the women, both married and unmarried, who have voluntarily chosen to live childless? Church officials have not known what to do with this group. What does one say to the thousands of women who defy convention and choose to remain childless because they feel this is the option that best suits them?

For centuries there have been women, married and single, who have opted to remain as what in medical parlance is called *nullipara*, a nonmother (there is no parlance for the nonfather). In my travels I have met many women who have chosen for a variety of reasons not to have children: adventure, romance, education, spirituality, art, idealism, duty, poverty, terror, or because they couldn't see how they would be able to strike a balance between their love for their work and all that would be required of them if they chose to become a mother. The other Marys in Scripture—Mary Magdalene and Mary of Bethany—come to mind to help symbolize for us life as a *nullipara*, the woman without progeny but not without contribution. Married women were customarily introduced as "wife of . . . ," but on occasion a woman appears in Scripture who defies the norm. Mary of Magdala, also known as Mary Magdalene, sacrificed domesticity to be a part of Jesus' ministry and is singled out along with other women for making material sacrifices on behalf of the ministry (Luke 8:2). Likewise, Mary of Bethany, sister of Martha and Lazarus, abandoned the traditional feminine role of the entertaining hostess and perfect housekeeper for the chance to soak up Jesus' teachings uninterruptedly. Even though the two single and childless Marys have for centuries won a place in the hearts of women for their individuality and unconventionality, it can't be denied that the biblical writers celebrated being a wife and a mother as the divinely ordained *essential* roles for women. Demographic studies over the last twenty years, however, show a decline in the number of available marriageable men, making it pretty certain that marriage and motherhood will not be in every woman's future.

Some years ago, when in my twenties, I wrote an essay entitled "Letter to an Unborn Child" and included it in a book I later wrote in my thirties about blessings and betrayals. It was a letter to an imaginary daughter, a daughter I never expected to have. She had lingered in my imagination for years as an alter ego as well as a constant companion. Given the way my love life was going back then and the amount of energy I had to expend to keep my career headed in the right direction, I was certain that marrying and having a child were not going to be a part of my future. I wrote my imaginary daughter (having a son was unimaginable to me even back then) asking her to forgive me for repeatedly choosing the wrong men for myself and for choosing career and adventure over her. I was fated to remain childless for the rest of my life, I reasoned.

Reading that letter now, twenty years after writing it and more than ten years after publishing it, I am embarrassed by the melodrama of it all. But then, my twenties were full of melodrama and passion, which explains why I was always in and out of relationships with men, never quite satisfied with the direction my life was taking, always volleying back and forth between emotional highs and lows, and always beating my breasts in my journals imploring God to save me, rescue me, protect me from myself. Ah, the drama of my twenties. I was too unstable to raise a child (and knew it) and too high-strung to settle down in love (which I didn't know then). Ten years later I did fall in love, marry, and have a baby—and I was (and continue to be) as surprised as anyone by the turn of events. For thirty-nine years I was no child's mother and was a pretty sorry prospect for the job, I must admit. But eight years now into motherhood and loving every moment of it, I still remember the stinging remarks and glances I received as a single childless woman, especially from religious women, when I let it be known that no, I didn't have children and quite frankly couldn't imagine them in my future. The horror and shock on their faces made it clear that in the eyes of some, I was at best a pitiful excuse for a woman, a selfish monster at worst. "Don't you *want* children?" someone would ask me with a tone akin to the tone used by a loved one peering into the face of a family member with a terminal illness, questioning the instructions of the terminally ill not to be kept alive by extraordinary measures should she flat-line: "Don't you *want* to live?" Like, *What's wrong with you?* My answer then is the same answer now, even with a child of my own. Nothing's wrong with a woman who, by choice or chance, is childless. Honor her if it's her choice. Plenty of women give birth to children every day who don't want them, don't take the time to care for them, women who resent their children and leave them for others to find them and take them. Honor the woman for knowing herself well enough to realize what she needs and doesn't need. Hug her and give her permission to grieve in your arms if she desires a child, but fate has it that she's unable to conceive a child. Sometimes we get to choose, sometimes we don't.

Just think how different the story of Mary and Elizabeth might have been if it were more like the world in which we live. Suppose Elizabeth had never been able to conceive. Imagine the lessons awaiting us if upon discovering that she was pregnant, Mary had hastened to visit her infertile cousin simply because she was a wise, comforting friend. But, of course, Elizabeth did conceive. The reason Elizabeth finds her way into the story of Mary is *because* she did eventually conceive, and the son she bore, John the Baptist, grew up to become the prophetic forerunner to Mary's son Jesus. But what if Elizabeth had remained barren? What if, too, the angel Gabriel had found Mary and informed her that her divinely ordained duty was to remain childless and celibate for the remainder of her life? In that case, a celibate Mary seeks Elizabeth for advice on how to break her betrothal to Joseph.

Can two women reach out to each other and find satisfying companionship if one of the women is pregnant and the other permanently unable to bear a child? It's possible. Part of what it means to grow up as a woman and to start looking at the world and your own life with new eyes is to cease being quick to pass judgment on those who have chosen a path different from your own. You learn to accept the choices other women have made, for you know how much courage it takes to choose one path and how much pain and guilt you face when you must turn your back on the path you didn't choose. While the two of you may have bonded together in the beginning because both of you were pregnant at the same time or both of you were raising small children, or because you were both married and the two wives and two husbands befriended each other, the older you get, the less important having children and having husbands becomes to the staying power of women's friendships.

Lasting friendships between women are those

where the parties stick by each other's sides through and despite the fortunes and misfortunes of marriage, children, finances, careers, health, and the like. We learn to rejoice over the other's good fortune, and to let our friendships help us survive the crushing blows of disappointment and loss. Their mutual experience of finding themselves impossibly blessed by God, one pregnant without the benefit of intercourse and the other pregnant in old age, brought the two women together in Luke 1:39–56. But once they came together, it was the woman-to-woman sharing, praying, and dreaming about the women they would one day become that bonded them forever. Whatever path a woman chooses with regard to childbearing, she will need the support of other women. The scorn and punishment that society heaps on those who refuse to conform to the biological expectation that women breed means that every woman must find the inner strength to decide what's best for her and to accept the things that are beyond her power to change. With that, let those of us with children honor our sisters who do not have children, both the ones whose reproductive choices are different from our own and those who struggle to make their peace with the fact that they had no choice in the matter.

*Lord, help me not confuse a woman's womb
with her soul.
With her who has given birth I rejoice.
With her who chooses not to bear I celebrate her right
to choose a different path for herself.
As for my sister who had no choice, I stand in
solidarity, lending her my shoulder for support.
Show us all the other different ways to create,
nurture, and reproduce good in the world,
without having babies.
Show us how to love and raise the babies
we already have.
Teach us how to create a world of
love and justice for all
where no child is left behind,
and no mother, or mother's friend, is made ashamed.*

Late Bloomers

Compared to her cousin Mary, Elizabeth was what today we might call a "late bloomer." After years of slow, quiet gestation, the dormant bulb of her identity finally began to send up sturdy shoots and fragrant blossoms. When others her age were giving birth, becoming mothers, discovering the joys of childbirth, raising their children, Elizabeth was looking on. Perhaps you know how Elizabeth felt. Perhaps you know what it is to feel underdeveloped, flat, and stuck in one spot compared to what's taking place in the lives of those around you. While others seem always clear about who they are and what they want and know how to go after it, you are always wrestling with feelings of insecurity and low self-esteem. All those years listening on the phone as one girlfriend talked about yet another job she was quitting, and the new job she was lining up for herself that would begin next month, the pay raise she was planning to negotiate and get on this new job, this new career path which she was confident was the right one for her (from your count, her fourth in five years), you've felt like a stick-in-the-mud by comparison. There you were, with more experience and degrees than her, but unable to imagine yourself voluntarily leaving one job without another one already nailed down. And even after ten years on the job, you haven't been able to bring yourself to speak up and ask for the raise you know you deserve. As you sat congratulating your girlfriend, you found yourself secretly envying her courage and sense of initiative. And as another girlfriend held you glued to your restaurant chair as she talked about taking a break from love affairs, kicking her last live-in boyfriend out of her apartment, spending some time with herself, traveling alone, your spine froze just trying to imagine the strength and feeling of self-worth you would need to break off the affair you were having with your married coworker.

Late bloomer. Perhaps that's what you are. You are not slow, it just takes you longer. Your friends aren't better women than you. They are just swifter at changing things around than you are. But it's the end result that counts. Late bloomers bloom later, not never. Eventually, after years of making and breaking promises to themselves to change some things about their life, late bloomers take the hint and start moving things around. "The race is not to the swift," so says the famous proverb. Here I'll paraphrase the second half of it to say, "but to whoever eventually hits her stride and sees everything through to a fulfilling ending." Don't count yourself out. Late bloomers still have a chance.

Late bloomers are those who finally stop becoming and start being, stop surviving and start thriving, stop settling for less and start demanding what they deserve. Elizabeth was a late bloomer like so many of us. As concerned as she was for Mary and the awesome responsibility the angel had placed upon her at such a young and tender age, Elizabeth probably found herself wondering as she sat with Mary those three months how different her own life would have been had she become pregnant when other women her age were having their babies. In some ways, Mary was blessed to have her whole life ahead of her. Elizabeth could have felt old and used up next to Mary. She may have looked at the warm glow in Mary's skin and compared it to the dull shine of her own, and found herself wondering, *Where did all the years go? If I had know then what I know now.*

In some other ways, however, Elizabeth felt she was the luckier one. What she'd lost in youth, she'd gained in wisdom. A side of her was glad for all those years of not knowing, not understanding, and having to grope in the dark for her way. It made being pregnant in her late years that much sweeter. She was old enough to appreciate babies, giving birth, watching yourself change before your own eyes. She had stayed in seclusion those first five months of her pregnancy not because she was afraid of what was happening to her or what others were saying. She stayed in seclusion *because* she understood what was going on and because she knew what others were saying. As a late bloomer, she was older and wise enough to know how to protect herself from those whose meddling comments could cause her to miscarry what God was birthing in her.

Everyone is a late bloomer in one way or another. If you know what it is to toil away in relative obscurity for many years, kept from reaching your full potential by others whose embrace ended up being a strangle, hampered by fear and feeling unworthy, then feeling yourself blasting into the galaxy later in life with passion and commitment—then you know what it means to be a late bloomer. Some late bloomers are those who may have had a "successful" first career, the career they chose when they were in their twenties, and one day found themselves taking down the shingle and throwing in the towel for the chance to bloom again in a new career, more meaningful work. A "calling" is what you're after now, a vocation you feel pulled to, one that better suits the person you've become in your late thirties, forties, and beyond. You no longer wonder whether you can do it, you are too busy planning how you are going to do it.

What do you know today about God and yourself that you didn't know and couldn't have known ten, twenty, thirty, forty years ago? Those ten, twenty, thirty, or forty years weren't a total waste. Like Elizabeth, you were learning what you needed to learn. While others were scurrying about, pretending to know exactly what they wanted, you were learning some things about commitment, devotion, dependability, loyalty, prayer, and trust. Though it may seem otherwise, God never forgot you. It felt as though everyone else was passing you by. You felt left. But you weren't. You were on schedule, God's schedule. Your friends who were marrying, having babies, changing jobs, changing husbands and lovers, weren't better, smarter, faster learners than you. They were just living their lives as best as they knew how. And you stayed put and laid dormant because that was who you were. But that was then, and this is now. Before, you wondered if you would ever change; from now on, you will be wondering if you will ever stop changing.

Late bloomers can blossom in their twenties or as late as their eighties. In fact, it's never too late to be a late bloomer. All it takes is for you to find it in yourself to tell the truth about what your life has been like: *I've been scared all my life, but now I'm not afraid anymore. All these years I went around thinking everyone else's life was more exciting than my life, and that something was wrong with me. But I don't think that anymore.*

I'm just a late bloomer. Celebrate your blooms *because* they took so long in coming. Be grateful for that second wind. Relish the learning and wisdom you've garnered. This is your season, Elizabeth. Seize it. Give birth to the gift of God within you. You've now got talent *and* the inner strength that comes with age. You've now got enthusiasm *and* the wisdom that comes with experience. You're ready. Take a stanza from Jenny Joseph's highly acclaimed poem, "Warning." In that poem a woman looks forward to growing old enough to throw away constraint, pick flowers from other people's gardens, learn to spit, and have a fine time. The poem begins with these lines:

> *When I am an old woman I shall wear purple*
> *With a red hat which doesn't go, and doesn't suit me.*

What kind of woman do you imagine yourself growing into becoming? If you're in your twenties now, what kind of woman do you want to be in your thirties? If you're thirty-something now, who do you want to be in your forties? If you're in your forties like I am, what single characteristic do you most want to carry with you into your fifties? Who is the woman you're dreaming of becoming at sixty-something? seventy-something? when at last you grow into an old woman?

"When I turn fifty, I want to be me," a friend leaned over and whispered to me at the fiftieth birthday celebration of a mutual friend. "Who are you now?" I whispered back. "A figment of my husband's imagination, my children's imagination, a figment of my own imagination, I think sometimes." Knowing that her fiftieth birthday was coming up in six months, I responded, "Well, you'd better get started letting her have more speaking parts to play, 'cause it looks like she's scheduled to have a starring role before the year is over."

As for me, when I turn fifty, I want to be outrageous. Perhaps I should start practicing now being outrageous so that in three years my family and friends won't think I've lost my mind when I finally start saying and doing everything that comes to my mind. Better late than never. Meet me with your purple dress and red hat on.

It took a little while,
putting down roots here, only to rip them up later on,
trying this spot in this garden and then another,
too long in the sun here,
overshadowed by others over there.
Finally I found my spot,
it was not too late for me.
The Master Gardener plucked me up and put me
where I could get

just enough water, just enough sun.
Now watch me bloom.
Just because I'm scared today doesn't mean that I'll be
scared tomorrow.
You should have seen me yesterday.
Before God replanted me.

Mary and Red Shoes

I still remember those red patent leather shoes. It was love at first sight. I had to have them the moment I saw them in the store. I whined and sniffled and pouted until my poor father, who knew nothing about shopping for shoes for a four-year-old girl, gave in and bought them for me. Never mind that the shoes were a size too small. The last pair of girls' red patent leather shoes of the season were lying there on the rack all shiny and bright, and I was smitten. I tried them on, and it was magic. I knew then and there that I was born to wear red patent leather shoes. My mother would never have allowed it, but she was in the hospital with my new baby sister. I had two days with my shoes before she would be released. With no salesman on duty at the discount store to measure my feet and alert my father that my little toes were stuffed into the plastic leather, my father took my four-year-old word that they fit. "Yes, Daddy, I can wear them," I said, looking up pleadingly into his eyes. My father didn't know any better, and I didn't care that my toes ached. I gladly suffered for the chance to walk out of that store with glossy-looking red Easter shoes. And suffer I did.

My feet hurt for two days. But that didn't stop me from prancing around the house in my new red shoes. I woke up and went to bed at night with them on my feet. That went on for two days until my mother arrived home with my new baby sister, Joyce. The moment I ran out the door to greet my mother with my new red shoes clicking across the pavement, my mother knew. "Why did you buy shoes too small for the child?" my mother shot at my father as she stepped out of the car. "They fit, Mommy," I protested, "they don't hurt." But my mother could tell the moment she saw me skipping gingerly across the pavement and into her arms that something was not right. The sight of my toes curled up in the shoe gave me away. "Take those shoes back to the store," she said, more to my father than to me. "But they were the last red shoes," I protested, tears welling in my eyes. But my mother, being the sensible type, wouldn't hear of it. With a new baby bringing the number of children in the house to four, there was no money to squander on shoes that didn't fit. Even beautiful red patent leather shoes. I cried for four days. I vowed not to have anything to do with the new baby just to hurt my mother.

But that didn't last. Days passed, but I never forgot the red patent leather shoes that fit my imagination if not my feet. Years later I continue to be drawn to red shoes. The moment I try them on, a warning goes off inside me. *Be careful of wearing red shoes,* I hear as I slide my feet into a pair, *they have the power to break your heart.*

Some women live their whole lives resisting the urge to wear red shoes. Others of us cannot. We try them on anyway, knowing full well the dangers. But there's also the magic, the joy, the adventure, the risk of happiness that we can't resist. They might just fit this time. Perhaps of all the other girls in Nazareth, Galilee, and beyond, Mary was chosen to be the mother of Jesus because she wasn't afraid of her own gift. She was apprehensive about where it might all lead. But that's not the same as being unsure of your Self.

Imagine my surprise some years ago when browsing in a bookstore I came upon a Hans Christian Andersen story, "The Red Shoes," about a little girl obsessed with and possessed by a pair of red shoes that send her into a dancing fit and ultimately lead her to a tragic end. I understood immediately the little girl's obsession with her shoes, and knew firsthand the shoe's magical powers over a little girl's hunger for adventure. The basic storyline of "The Red Shoes" did not begin with Andersen. He adapted the popular tale, as he did most of the stories he is famous for, and gave it his own ethnic wit and imaginative twist. It hints of an old wives' tale, a story one imagines women passed down to their daughters, about what happens when a girl's wild ways go unchecked. In the story, red comes to symbolize life and sacrifice. It's the kind of story every woman knows without realizing that she knows it. It is every story we've ever heard about suppressing the outrageous woman within. Just beneath a love for red dancing shoes may lie latent a volcano of other obsessions, unmet needs, secret fantasies, and deep longings. Take the shoes from the shelf and give in to the urge to try them on, and there's no telling what may happen. You may not be able to take them off. You may never be able to go back to being who you were. One obsession may lead to another. You may become unrecognizable to yourself and to others. Leave those red shoes where they are. Don't trust urges you can't explain. Don't give in to impulses that make no sense.

Why do some women manage to grow out of perpetual girlhood while others never do? Why is it that some women, like me, can't stand to see a pair of red shoes with no feet stuck down in them, while others resist the urge to try on the red shoes dangling from the shoe rack? Why do some women learn to ride out the seas of change, uncertainty, and unknowing and go on to grow, mature, and create new meaning for themselves in the midst of it all, while others give up before they get started, or faint midway, or pretend that nothing's stirring or bubbling inside, threatening to erupt? There is no simple answer to any of these questions. People are complex. One thing's for sure, however: There are good reasons why some women sleep through their own revolution. We are put to sleep early on as girls, and if we're not careful, sleep can extend throughout life, leaving us unconscious and numb at just about the time when we're supposed to be transforming into butterflies.

"Sit down."

"Be quiet."

"Be nice."

"Smile."

"Get back in line."

"Stop laughing so loudly."

"Fix yourself up."

"Mind your manners."

"Cross your legs."

"Stop acting like a boy."

They meant us no harm. They thought they were helping us, getting us ready for life. Training us for our script as girls. They assured us that if we sat quietly, minded our manners, and looked pretty, spoke softly, and kept our thoughts to ourselves, we would get ahead, get the attention we wanted, and be rewarded. Wanting to please, we tried to do as they instructed. But then we grew up and became women. And we kept waiting. And nothing happened. Or what did happen wasn't what we expected to happen. And we found ourselves at thirty, forty, fifty, and beyond trying to find our voice, trying to speak up, trying to find the courage to stand up for ourselves and not bother with what other people thought. Trying to find the courage to get out of line. It can take a lifetime of unlearning. But it can be done. It usually begins with small steps. Speak up. Stop saying you don't know when you do know.

But what if you take the red shoes from the shelf, try them on, and you can't take them off? What if in a dancing fit they lead you to parts unknown and unde-sired and unsafe for you? It's dangerous out there for women. Ask Hagar. Ask Jephthah's daughter. Ask the woman caught in adultery. Ask Ruth and Naomi. Ask Vashti. Ask Mary, who faced execution if she was de-ceiving Joseph about how she became pregnant. Isn't the story about the red shoes one told to warn daugh-ters about becoming too enthralled with something and spinning out of control? Yes and no. Yes, it is about the dangers of living life without boundaries. But the story of the red shoes is more particularly about a woman's lack of instinct to create boundaries. The girl in the story is every woman who doesn't know that ex-cesses can dull your instinct for self-care. She doesn't know when enough is enough. When the young girl saw how gracefully and effortlessly she danced with the shoes on, she couldn't resist their powers and sneaked them on her feet when the old woman guardian wasn't looking. The old woman had succeeded in wresting them away from the child earlier and had placed them on a shelf the child wasn't supposed to be able to reach. But the child managed to get them down anyway. The old woman warned the little girl about the shoes. But the child couldn't resist. Her defenses were down, and she didn't listen to her own inner voice telling her that if she wasn't careful, the shoes' powers could become self-destructive.

The difference between you and the woman whose life you envy most is that despite her fears she took the red shoes off the shelf and tried them on anyway. And before the shoes could get the best of her, she ran instinctively to Elizabeth's house for lessons on dancing and harnessing the power of red shoes. For centuries the virtuous woman has been the woman who has stifled her own powers and denied the gifts God has given her for fear of offending others. No one told her that with mentoring and a few instructions, she wouldn't have to cut off her own feet to please those around her. It's possible to stay on your feet dancing, without breaking every bone in your body.

The moment my mother saw me skipping, more like hobbling, out to meet her in my new red shoes, she could tell something was wrong. She knew I was in pain, although I was also in denial. She knew that shoes that don't fit will ultimately deform the feet. I protested. I denied. I sulked. But she knew better. She didn't argue with my four-year-old choice of red patent leather shoes for Easter. She smiled when she saw how much her little four-year-old revered the shoes, and she took a bit of delight, I believe, in watching me prance about from room to room in them as I followed her with the baby. But after a few hours she laid down the law. She wasn't putting up with shoes that could potentially deform her daughter's feet.

As I've already pointed out, every woman needs a mothering presence, an accountability partner (or partners) who help you see what you can't see by yourself. You need someone who'll say to you, "Dance in your red shoes, baby, but be sure you got a pair that fit your soul." For me, it was my mother. For Mary, it was Elizabeth. For Ruth, it was Naomi. Mary had her sister Martha. Do you have someone who is happy for your new shoes but who knows that there's a difference between you wearing the shoes and the shoes wearing you out?

Artistically gifted women are especially susceptible to the seduction of red shoes. We are susceptible because we are always hungry, hungry for truth, hungry to see behind the lies, hungry to create, hungry to share what we see and feel. A large part of re-creating oneself and giving birth to new selves is learning how to tap into the creativity welling up inside and trying to figure out what to pour it into. You look around and you see brilliant colors of red, purple, orange, yellow, blue, and green everywhere. The world is on fire with possibility. Reading biographies lately on one of my favorite jazz-blues singers, Billie Holiday, I am convinced that here was a woman who shared my love for red shoes. I could see in her story a woman who should have left the shoes on the shelf. But it wasn't the singing in the end that did in the soul of this creatively gifted woman who could make your heart stop when she lit into one of her slow-burning torch songs. Nor was it even the alcohol, the heroin addiction, the cigarettes, the fist-fighting brawls she was prone to, or the string of abusive, exploitative men she fell for. It was her lack of internal alarm to warn her when she was in danger. Not just physical danger. In fact, one thing that's clear from reading police reports on her arrests was that she was a scrappy sort who had no qualms punching policemen who insulted her, lovers who took their fists to her face, or women who slept around with her men. It seems that she was gutsy about protecting everything but her own inner well-being. She didn't know how to protect her soul from danger. Listening to her music more than fifty years after her death, you wish a tune like "Solitude," which she delivers with yearning, had as its focus a woman celebrating the renewal and gathering of one's many selves, a woman delighting in being able to enjoy the solitude of her own thoughts. Instead, Holiday's "Solitude" is about a woman who pines away for a love that's gone bad.

> *In my solitude you haunt me*
> *with memories of days gone by.*
> *In my solitude you taunt me*
> *with memories that never die. . . .*
> *In my solitude I'm friendless.*
> *Dear Lord above, send back my love.*

How much longer might we have had the musical genius of Billie Holiday with us had she known how to harness the power of the shiny, powerful red shoes and wear them for her benefit? What if she hadn't been afraid of solitude? I mean that kind of solitude that empties you of the need to be seen, to please others, and to walk the streets at night in search of a man that has left you for good. It's a lesson all pregnant virgins have to learn. That is, how to wear your red shoes and not let them wear you *out*. With their shiny, magical color, their powerful, potent, choreographic power, can also come behavior, people, and seductions that gradually chip away at your spiritual bones—first the tiny bones, then the larger ones. Eventually your entire inner framework collapses and there's nothing left inside to help you stand upright.

Fortunately, Mary's story ends on a positive note. She goes on to grow into a strong, caring, committed mother who stands watch over her son's ministry throughout his life. Her son eventually dies. But she goes on to become the paradigmatic mother of the New Testament church. But we need to know that not every story about a woman who takes her dreams in her hands ends on a positive note. Some women crash under the burden of the gift God has given them.

But even the lives of women like Billie Holiday can teach us something. We can learn from the living and the dead, the good role models and the tragic role models, pious women and women with no spiritual center. When you're on the verge, like the Blessed Virgin Mary, of creating a new life, obsessed with the new thing that's growing within you, you are like the little girl in the story of the red shoes—you need a center. Someplace you can always come back to. An inner compass that defies the gravitational pull of everything around you and keeps you headed in the right direction. Something more wondrous and mysterious than the bright red shoes that have you in their grip. You need to have the gift of God's love within you.

To protect yourself against the darker powers of your new shiny red shoes, you also need people around you to help you make the right choices. They walk with you through the changes taking place in your life. They offer you support, a listening ear, a word of prayer, morsels of encouragement as you struggle to hear clearly what God is saying. They are happy when you finally come upon your red shoes, and laugh and celebrate with you as you try on one new pair of red shoes after another, trying to find the pair that fits just so. They don't try to talk you out of wearing red shoes. But they do have your permission to tell you when your defenses are down, your instincts are a bit blurred, and the shoes are making you spiral out of control.

Years of repeatedly stuffing your true feelings inside, pretending that any man is better than no man at all, relying upon drugs and alcohol to dull the pain or to relive a moment in the past when you felt most alive, gradually erode your natural God-given instinct to sense when you're in danger of losing yourself and in danger of losing the creative gifts God gave you. There was more music in Billie Holiday. But she died in 1959 at the ripe age of forty-four, just about the time when most creative women are ready to give birth to their true genius.

I'm grateful that my mother knew instinctively, despite my protests, that I couldn't wear the red shoes my father bought for me and insisted that I take them off and send them back. If she hadn't, the shoes may have eventually warped my young, growing feet. Thank you, Mom, if you're reading this from above. Thank you for paying attention. Thank you for sensing when your daughter was in danger. Thank you for teaching me how not to cram my feet in shoes that don't fit; and even if they did fit in the beginning, how to take them off and pack them off when they fit no longer. I'm still learning. I'm still a sucker for red shoes. But like the Blessed Virgin Mary, I'm learning how to surround myself with people who see what I can't see and who can teach me a thing or two about how to dance the night away without breaking my neck in the process.

I'm still learning
how to listen,
how to distinguish what feels good to me
from what is good for me.
I'm still learning.
Teach me, Lord, how to dance in red shoes without
spinning out of control.
And how to trust the voice
from deep within
when she says, "Enough."

Something Within

I had heard his voice before. The man in the third row accused me of being harsh in what I'd had to say about the church during a speaking engagement. He accused me of being radical in my vision of what I thought it would take to restore right relations between God, creation, and human beings. I was, according to him, hysterical. He didn't use those words exactly, but that's what he was saying. Ten years ago I would have frozen up when a man like him stood to tell me, "Get back in line. Take off those red shoes. Smile. Stop being unreasonable. How dare you!" But that was ten years ago. This is now. I like my red shoes. They fit. I've learned how to wear them to my benefit. I'm not afraid of men like him, nor of my red shoes, anymore. "Obviously we see the world differently, sir. But thank you for your comments. Next."

One day you stop being scared. One day you stop crying. One day you stop caring what other people think. One day you refuse to go back to being the timid, silent, apologetic, self-doubting woman who prefaced everything she had to say with, "Maybe I'm wrong but . . ." If you're Mary, one day you move from self-doubt ("How can this be?") to glorious rejoicing and praise (the Magnificat). One day you find yourself saying, "Even if I'm wrong (and I don't think I am), this is what I think. . . ." But what does it take for that day to come about?

If you're Elizabeth, you come out of hiding. "The moment I heard the sound of your greeting, the babe in my womb leapt for joy!" she said with exclamation. Something in Elizabeth quickened when she heard Mary's greeting. The baby in her flipped and did a somersault. Everything fell into place. Mary's voice and the child within clicked. What the past six months she'd only suspected and hoped was true was at last confirmed. She wasn't just pregnant, she was free. There was nothing to be ashamed of. Elizabeth was free to let the new woman come out of hiding.

Elizabeth is like you and me. One day your inner world and outer world click and come together. The invitation comes and you are ready to accept it. The offer to take a job in a new city comes, and you take it. The chance to vacation alone in Bali comes along, and you jump at it. The door opens for you to start a book club, and you go for it. The idea to convert that spare bedroom into a prayer and meditation room for you returns, and this time you decide that the time has come for your adult son to stand on his own feet. *It's time. It begins to come together.* You are ready for you. The tumblers in the lock finally line up to make the right clicking sound, the lock at last unlocks after years of trying, and all the treasure within comes spilling out of you and into your lap.

The sound of Mary's voice awakened things lying dormant in Elizabeth. Elizabeth had heard the sound of her cousin's voice scores of times before. There had been plenty of times, no doubt, when as an older girl cousin, Elizabeth had been stuck with caring for her younger cousins as the women of the family gathered on the other side of the house slaughtering animals, boiling water, and cooking over outdoor fires. But Elizabeth wasn't pregnant back then, so the sound of Mary's voice calling Elizabeth's name had no effect. Conversely, for six months now she'd been pregnant, but there had been no sign of Mary anywhere. There had been no contact between the two women since Elizabeth conceived. But the moment Mary entered the house and called Elizabeth's name, everything came together. The baby leapt, and Elizabeth knew what she'd only suspected. The woman she was before was now gone. Something within announces the new you and lets you know that it's time.

"How can you be so sure?" you're asking. To those who insist that it has never come together for them, that their life has always been out of sorts, that things have always taken place too soon, too late, or never at all, and that there's never been an "Aha!" moment for them, I reply, "How can you be so sure?" Can it be that you have missed such moments? Could it be that there were times when you were so preoccupied with what was going on outside you, or what you were feeling on the inside, that you never managed to take advantage of either? Sometimes it hurts to focus. Some women never find the courage to summon what they know is right and use it to change the course of their lives. They can do it for others, but they can't do it for themselves. It feels selfish. It means taking themselves too seriously. It costs too much.

Other women figure it out. Like the professional thief, they learn how to lean close, put their ears to the lock, and listen to the tumblers for the right sound when all the elements come together. They learn how to steal themselves away from all the forces in society, church, family, and themselves that have tried to silence them. They figure out the combination of divine waiting and human motivation, solitude and communion, listening for God and acting on experience, fulfilling duties and finding fulfillment in yourself. All the information you need is there waiting for you. It's a matter of seizing the moment when you hear Mary's greeting and learning how to dive deep within yourself for the answer. Mary's voice may come in the form of your daughter's question, "Mom, why do you stay and put up with all this?" Perhaps she speaks to you through the title of a book, a book you left there on the shelf at the store, but its title you can't get out of your head, *Imagine a Woman in Love with Herself.** Or perhaps Mary's voice comes through in a Scripture you've heard all your life, but this time you heard it differently. "The cover of the basket was lifted, and there in the basket a woman was sitting. . . ." (Zech. 5:7). Whatever it took, you heard her this time. It was like the missing key, the lost combination, the one last yank at the lock. All the wisdom you've gained over the years is stored somewhere deep within you, in the same room where all the prayers you've prayed are stored. There in that room where lessons are learned, insights gained, dreams dreamed, and prayers prayed, dwells God, who waits to help us put the pieces of the puzzle together. Before you know it, and before you can silence her, a voice within you yells back at the top of her spiritual lungs, saying, *Yes, I hear you!*

*Patricia Lynn Reilly, *Imagine a Woman in Love with Herself* (Conari Press, 1999).

When I am tempted to doubt myself
and question my gifts and experience,
remind me, God, of all that I know,
and that which I don't know that I know.
Remind me who I am, and
whose I am.
Even when I hide behind my piety to avoid doing what
must be done,
and use you as an excuse for indecision, for lack of
action,
for silencing myself.
Love me enough to lift the lid off my basket,
order me to stop crouching in the dark,
like a woman without a God.

Surprised by Passion

$\mathcal{Q}$uickly, name something you enjoy doing so much that once you get started, all your focus, energy, and intellect are absorbed by it. You lose all sense of time, and when you're done, you leave spent, happy, and itching to get back to it. That's your passion.

Quickly, name someone you know whom you admire for the enthusiasm, zeal, and commitment they bring to everything they do. Could it be that you are drawn to this person because he or she has passion?

We all know what it's like to feel physical passion for someone. Which explains why the moment the word "passion" is used, the first thing that comes to mind is sexual passion. We think of passion as a sensation. Passion can be expressed in different ways, however. For example, one of my passions is writing. When the thoughts in my head finally flow through my typing and affix themselves onto my computer screen, a part of me leaps from my chair and yells, *Yes! That's what I'm trying to say.* Or more accurately, *Yes! That's what I've been hearing but haven't been able to get right until after all these attempts.* It is the joy of accomplishing something I've tried unsuccessfully to do in the past, and finally getting it right.

Writing is one of my passions. But there are others. Ask about the passion I find in spending time with my husband, in raising my daughter, in sitting across a restaurant table from a dear friend, journaling, sitting on my screened porch relishing my quiet time with God, reclining in bed with a good book. There's no one kind of passion. There are as many different kinds of passions as there are experiences that cause you to stretch, to risk something, to best yourself, to lose yourself, and to succeed against the odds. One thing about each experience—you never stop being surprised by passion when it overtakes you. It's as though you've never known passion until that moment. No matter how many times you've felt it before, it's a totally humbling experience every time. At last, I did it, he did it, she did it, we made it, God smiled on us all.

One of the reasons passion is quickly equated with sex is that both can be "out-of-body" experiences and both draw on our energy, enthusiasm, deep concentration, and a fair amount of fantasy to transport us to another realm of reality. We live in a time when our sex life is the barometer for determining how fulfilled we are. According to this kind of logic, the better the sex you're having, the better your life is. You see then why sex in some ways has become the new spirituality and the new religion of contemporary society, the bearer of most people's hopes of encountering something truly "other." But lasting passion is not the result of physical pleasure and stimuli. Rather, passion is an inner source of energy that flows out into every aspect of your being. It is not something you possess. You don't *have* passion. You don't *get* passion. You don't even find passion. Passion finds and possesses you, once you relax and surrender yourself to it, and let what you don't know you know come to the surface. Passion happens to you when you let go of your need to be in control.

Elizabeth was overcome at the sound of Mary's voice. She felt humbled. She felt blessed. She knew at that moment that she was part of something larger, and was grateful for the good fortune to be included: "Why has this happened to me that the mother of my Lord should come to me?" Hearing Mary's voice was just what Elizabeth needed after months of uncertainty. She wasn't so much ashamed of being a pregnant woman as much as she was uncertain whom she could turn to to share her good fortune. That's the interesting thing about passion. Not everyone shares your passion. They want to, but they can't. They are too mired in their own unhappiness, and too fixed upon being in control, to allow themselves to be transported by your good fortune. But something about the lilt in Mary's voice and her good-natured laughter told Elizabeth that at last she was safe. Here was someone who shared her passion for life. Because passion is contagious, Mary's enthusiasm for all the new and wondrous things God was doing in her life awakened Elizabeth's passion for the same. "Deep calls to deep," says the psalmist. Ah, the sound of women embracing and reuniting after months apart. Emotions cannot be contained. The passion of shared memories, shared testimonies, and shared love overflow.

My husband excuses himself from the room when my girlfriends and I reunite after months of separation. He can't take the squeals, the laughter, the tears, the hugs followed by more squeals, laughter, and hugs. Most of all, he can't take all of us talking at the same time. He complains that he can't understand a word anyone is saying. But we don't have that problem. We hear and understand every word. He doesn't understand because he doesn't share the passion underlying our friendship. He doesn't share our (com)passion for each other's divorces, family deaths, breast cancer, restored marriages, promotions, public scandal, rebellious daughters, apathetic sons, new careers, growing wisdom. One of us bleeds, all of us bleed. One of us at last has cause for celebration, and we are on the phone squealing and passing the news to all with jubilation. I can imagine Zechariah bolting out the door when he heard Mary's and Elizabeth's squeals. He preferred the somber company of men to the sounds of female laughter coming from his house. Perhaps you know how Mary and Elizabeth felt as they fell into each other's arms. Ah, the comfort, the inexpressible joy of feeling safe with someone with whom you don't have to weigh your words, but can pour out your thoughts as they come, certain that unlike others, she knows how to sort the music from the babble.

When was the last time you were knocked completely off your feet by a friend's good news? What was your last surprisingly joyous experience? Are you and I really that old that nothing surprises us anymore, nothing makes us feel transported to another realm? I don't know about you, but I don't want to live so long that I lose my passion for living. Passion is born out of a commitment to live life to its fullest, knowing how to jump at the chance to join a celebration, being willing to mourn with those who mourn, and throwing yourself into every experience as if it's your last.

By nature each of us craves passion. We are drawn to passionate, charismatic people. Men sit in front of the television for hours watching sports, and women tape their favorite soap operas while at work, because both groups can't get enough of people who are so committed to their objectives, and so absorbed in what they are doing, that they will break all the rules to get their way. Looking back on it now, I'm sure that the fact that my favorite shoes from my childhood were red, the color of passion and life, contributed to my fascination with them. My red shoes gave me permission to feel and do things I otherwise wouldn't.

It's so easy to grow up and lose the passion we once had as kids. Part of being young was having the capacity to feel and express a wide range of emotions. No separation existed between one's body, feelings, and intellect. They were all one within us as girls. But then we grew into women, and suddenly we found ourselves being warned against becoming hysterical, emotional, loud, and irrational. A wedge was driven between our bodies, emotions, and intellect, and we became split at the root. We had to choose between being sensible and being passionate, or so it seemed. Sensible people make sensible choices. Passionate people lose their heads and make fools of themselves. We were told that we were too sensitive, too emotional, too expressive, too intense, and too unstable. We heard rumors about female colleagues who lost the respect of their male colleagues because they were too emotional. We watched our husbands back out of arguments on the grounds that we were too hysterical. We know mothers whose judgments about their children are suspect because they supposedly lack the necessary objectivity to evaluate their child rationally. So we learned to stifle it, keep it inside, keep a stiff upper lip, chill out, cool it, grow up. Our emotions became our enemy. Passion was confined to the bedroom. Feelings, however, are a gift from God. Essential to our physical and psychological health is our ability to feel and express a full range of emotions. Our immune systems depend upon our ability to express a range of emotions in order to keep our bodies functioning properly. Our bodies give us away when we can't express anger *and* joy *and* fear *and* sadness *and* hurt *and* love *and* the rest. The ability to be passionate is as essential to our well-being as the ability to feel sadness about something. There should be some area of our otherwise humdrum lives that makes us feel alive, out of control, stretched to the limit, full.

You're only half alive if sex is the only outlet you have for expressing passion. As delicious experiences as romance and lovemaking are, human nature cannot thrive on physical passion alone. The human body is wired so that over time, physical passion wanes and settles into manageable waves. In so doing, you finally get a chance to cultivate more lasting passions in your life. Hobbies. A true marriage. Talents. Friendships. Spiritual life. Lasting passion derives from the heart and spills over into your overall attitude about life in general. Passion drove Mary to Elizabeth's home. Mary wanted to understand; she wanted to make sense of what was happening to her; she wanted to be in the presence of someone else who knew what it was to be both excited and fearful about what God was doing in their lives. Above all, she longed to be with someone who had enough courage and curiosity about life to see their miracle through to its completion. That takes passion. Elizabeth's passion awakened at the sound of Mary's voice.

Some of the most passionate people I know are artists—poets, dancers, novelists, painters, singers, craftspeople, storytellers, even ministers. They know what it is to become completely absorbed in creating something, feeling so transported by the making and crafting of it, only to discover when the finished product is done and you're spent, that it isn't yours to own. You've glimpsed your true purpose, that which God created you to do, but you don't know if you could do it again. You're not sure if that same wild, wondrous, life-giving spirit it took to create it will return with the same force. Is there a word to describe what happens when a singer, after hours of practice, hits a note perfectly on opening night? Is there a paragraph that can explain the addiction to words that comes over a writer when she finally hits her stride in a novel? Is there a lexicon that aptly captures the joy that Mary and Elizabeth felt upon seeing each other? The joy of being in the presence of someone with whom you've forged a deep friendship, someone who is both a part of you and at the same time forever a mystery to you. What language is there for such a reality? What vocabulary can rightly express such an experience? Perhaps there is no language for describing what real passion is. You can only let yourself go and feel it with non-words.

The passion caused Mary to break out into in what has come to be known as the Magnificat. She began magnifying God and thanking God for her newfound purpose. It was a purpose she could only peek into now, but would take a lifetime to comprehend and live out. Elizabeth, inspired by a newfound passion, exclaimed, *Blessed are you among women, Mary, and blessed is the fruit of your womb . . . blessed is she who believes that what she has believed will come to pass.*

It took me a lifetime to understand the words to a song I grew up hearing the older people in my church singing: "This joy that I have, the world didn't give it and the world can't take away" says the old gospel hymn. It took me even longer to figure out that when they talked about joy, they were talking about passion. I didn't know enough about disappointment and misery back then to appreciate the joy they were talking about. Neither did I know enough about the inner well-being that comes with knowing that it is nothing but the love and dignity of God dwelling within that helps you survive life's disappointments with wholeness and joy. Those old people were well aware that God was the source of all passion. David the psalmist put it this way, "The joy [read "passion"] of the Lord is my strength."

Lord, it would have been enough if you'd brought joy.
It would have been enough if you'd brought happiness.
It would have been enough if you'd brought peace.
But I thank you for bringing laughter into my soul.
I never knew what I was missing.
Until laughter came into my soul.

Getting into the Dance

*Y*ou can't sing the words of the Magnificat—*My soul magnifies the Lord, and my spirit rejoices in God my Savior*—stiff and emotionless. You have to let go of all pretenses. You have to let go of your need to be in control. Forget trying to be dignified. This is not the prayer of an indifferent woman. She has found God within herself, and she can't help responding with her whole person—her heart, her mind, and her body. The woman who utters this prayer knows what it is to be touched deeply within her core, somewhere she's never tapped into before, and now that she has she feels more alive than ever.

If you've never been so jubilant about some good news or about some miracle taking place in your life that you wanted to jump and dance, then you have no way of empathizing with Mary's Magnificat. Who knows? What you may have been longing for all this time is just the right to feel what you feel and to be around people who respect your feelings. Mary had cause to celebrate. And so do you. If you don't know, you will someday. You may as well learn what to do now.

After months of struggling to break out of your cocoon, things are beginning to come together. You've met a friend who shares your passion. A few of your close loved ones are beginning to come around. For every two doors that had closed in your face, one has opened with your name on it. You had some lonely moments during these months, and it was all right. You learned this past year that you could survive being alone. Some blessings are cause for dancing. Let the passion rip, and get into the dance.

The prophet Miriam reached for a tambourine and bade the women around her to join her in giving thanks to God. They sang exuberantly to God on account of the miracle at the Red Sea: *Sing to the Lord, for the Lord has triumphed gloriously. The horse and the rider have been thrown into the sea.* Women have always been uninhibited about showing emotion. But many times we've done so at our own peril. We've been made to quell our feelings and question our intuitions. Some of us spend our whole lives doubting ourselves and being afraid of looking a fool. But Miriam and Mary would have none of that. Who wants to serve a God that doesn't make you want to dance from time to time? There is a saying, "Religion is not to be believed, it is to be danced." After all the dogma, precepts, rules, and creedal statements that formal religion tries to stuff down your throat, it all gets down to one question: What in your heart do you feel God is saying to you? What does your gut tell you? What do you keep hearing down in your soul? Go with that. Trust God. Trust your passion. Passion starts in the heart, and so does faith.

The Magnificat, so named because of the first line of Mary's praise (My *soul magnifies the Lord*) has been the subject of much comment over the centuries. Much of that comment has centered around what the Magnificat tells us about God. The Magnificat is also important because of what it tells us about Mary. The one thing least mentioned by others is the Magnificat's portrayal of Mary as a woman of deep passion. She expresses her gratitude to God for elevating her, a poor girl from the working-class town of Nazareth, for making her name known throughout the generations, for working wondrously on her behalf, and for doing so not only for her but for others like her as well. She was a woman of passion and compassion. She knew something every one of us has to learn: You can't want God to do something for you that you don't want God to do for others. Mary could be just as jubilant, emotional, and impassioned about what God was doing in the lives of Elizabeth, of all Israelites, and others, as she was about what God was doing on her behalf. The lesson here is to learn how to be happy for other people, and not for yourself alone. Celebrate with your friends over their good fortune. Be happy for your girlfriend when she marries before you, or conceives a baby when you're still trying. The joy you hope to reap in your life is tied to the joy you are able to plant in other people's lives.

I have one regret from my past. I never learned to dance. I was always too shy. I didn't trust my body. I was too self-conscious and inhibited to surrender my body to the music or to itself. I didn't want to make a fool of myself. I stayed away from parties much of my youth. Dancing requires a certain amount of trust—trusting your body, trusting your feelings, trusting the mood and the spirit to guide you and not betray you. I lacked that kind of trust. I suspect that I lost something from shying away from dancing. By never learning to dance, I never learned how to be spontaneous, emotional, uninhibited, and exuberant when the time comes to worship God. Like lots of other women, I have no qualms about yelling when I'm in pain or when I'm in danger. But I'm completely bashful and self-conscious about screaming out in joy and thanksgiving to God when the pain abates or the danger subsides. Five years ago I returned to class after thinking I'd never go back to school. This time the classes were different from those I took to get my graduate degrees. This time I took dance classes. I wanted to know what it felt like to worship, believe, and pray to God, like Miriam and Mary, with my whole person, with especially my body. I'm still no dancer. But that's all right. I dance what I can now at forty-something to make up for all those years when I refused to dance when it was easier and I was younger. Sometimes my body knows better than my mind what needs to be communicated to God.

Don't wait until it all makes sense to you before you praise God. Be grateful for what you already know. Let go of the need to be in control and to know every detail before you can trust God. There is a place in your spiritual journey when you have to trust God even when you can't track God. Be spontaneous. Stop trying to figure it all out. You have to trust your instincts. Trust your heart to guide you. Trust your passions. Let the inner woman have her say. You won't be sorry. She knows more than you think. She has information you need. She's been clamoring to get your attention. She's your gift from God. Every time you thank God for a little more wisdom and a little more insight, God sends you more. If you knew exactly where you were going, you wouldn't need to pray.

Mary burst into song and dance when she was pregnant and in a daze about all that was taking place in her life. When she still wasn't certain how it was going to turn out and what the future held, she let herself go, pulled her skirt up to allow for a few dance movements, and yelled at the top of her lungs, "My soul magnifies the Lord, and my spirit rejoices in God my Savior." A few months earlier she was stumbling in the dark, uncertain of anything other than that she couldn't go back to being her old self. All she knew for certain was that God had other plans for her. She was grateful for the little glimmer of insight. A friend who shared her passion. A companion who confirmed that she wasn't crazy. A mentor in whom she could confide. A purpose that was larger than anything she could have imagined for herself. A future that was surely in God's hands. It was enough to make her dance. Mary threw caution to the wind. She forgot for the moment about what she looked like, a pregnant woman carrying on so. I imagine her like Miriam before her, beckoning Elizabeth to join her. Imagine a circle of pregnant women jumping and giving God praise. Imagine women pregnant with new possibilities, laughing, falling all over themselves, dazed with new life, thanking God for seeing them this far along.

What do you have to be grateful for? What are you sitting there for? Get up and dance. Sometimes you have to put aside your sensible side and take the plunge. Lighten up and play a bit. Sometimes you have to throw being an adult to the wind, and play hopscotch, ride down the slide, take off your clothes and swim naked in the ocean. Sometimes you have to go

ahead and jump off the cliff, and let God show you
how to build your wings on the way down.

⚯

Lord God,
Dancer of the Universe,
show me how to dance.
Take my hand and give me a twirl.
Spin me around until I collapse in your arms.
Teach me a step until I get it right.
Lead me to where I'm not inclined to go on my own.
Toss me in the air until I squeal with delight
and can see further than I have ever seen before.
Make me dance with you
until I don't recognize my new Self
and I am breathless
with joy.